NANETTE

NANETTE

Edwards Park

Smithsonian Institution Press
Washington and London

B PARK

First time in paperback
Library of Congress Cataloging in Publication Data
Park, Edwards.
Nanette.
1. World War, 1939–1945—Campaigns—New Guinea.
2. World War, 1939–1945—Aerial operations,
American. 3. World War, 1939–1945—Personal
narratives, American. 4. Park, Edwards. 5. New
Guinea—History. 1. Title.
D767.P34 1977 813'.5'4 76–56445

ISBN 0-87474-737-6

Printed in the United States of America
97 96 95 94 93 92 91 90

British Library Cataloguing in Publication Data is available
The paper in this publication meets the requirements of the
American National Standard for Permanence of Paper for
Printed Materials Z39.48-1984

*Dedicated to
Nanette, of course. And to
all the people who worked
with me and with her and with
her sisters in those strange
old days. And to every old
machine that was ever endowed
with whatever it was. A soul,
maybe.
Also to my wife, who now
knows that she got me on
the rebound.*

Contents

Introduction

Practically everything in this book actually happened, so it's not really a novel. Yet these people and events have been altered, so you can't call it nonfiction. It's an Exaggeration.

Not exaggerated, however, is the bigotry of the 1940s, here expressed. The people of Gopher Squadron were racists and sexists. We felt some small guilt about the former, but not about the latter because we had never heard the word. To us, it was perfectly natural to think of women as, among many other things, sex objects, and to regard the machines we admired in terms we also applied to women.

That was the way we were.

NANETTE

I

The Sisterhood

Nanette was an airplane. That should be made clear right at
the start. She was not a very good plane; actually she
stank. But she did a lot for me, I realize, as I look back on her.

All the planes of that old war had distinguishing looks and
personalities. The P-40, the Kittihawk, was knobby and arro-
gant, a tomboy. The P-38, the Lightning, was lean and coltish,
a rich debutante. The P-47, the Thunderbolt, was massive and

dull, a peasant girl. The bombers had their distinctions, too, but I didn't know much about them.

Of all the fighters, two could really excite a flyer. One was the P-51, Mustang, lovely to look at, honest, efficient, hardworking and dependable. In those days she was thought of as a wife, and I know men who married her, back then, and are still in love with her. The other was the P-39, Airacobra. It was slim, with a gently curved tail section, a smoothly faired in air intake, and a perfectly rounded nose cone with its ugly, protruding cannon. But the Airacobra was lazy and slovenly and given to fits of vicious temper. It was a sexy machine, and rotten. Nanette was like that, and I was a little queer for her.

The ads in the magazines raved about the P-39, mostly because commercial artists liked to paint her. The ads raved about all warlike things, anyway—there would be a camouflaged howitzer or something, half hidden behind the big red Coke machine while soldiers stood around grinning at each other with white teeth and those tight-jawed faces that showed they were real American fighting men. On the back cover of *Fortune* there was a painting of a P-39 climbing steeply into the night sky. "Homesick Angel" said the copy, and went on to remind people how great American engineering was and how it turned out the world's finest equipment for the world's finest fighting man—GI Joe. Of course the ads pictured other planes, too, for the sake of corporate patriotism, but Homesick Angel I never forgot. Climbing a P-39 like that, at *night?* Christ, the thought makes me quiver with fright.

I first saw an Airacobra at Maxwell Field, Alabama, during preflight days as an army aviation cadet. She was sitting, sleek and deadly, at the corner of a rainswept airfield, looking like Rita Hayworth. I never realized that months later I would be entrusted with Nanette.

First I had to go through nine months of cadet training, during which I was retained simply because the nation was badly frightened by being in the war and concerned with getting every flier sufficiently qualified to get up there and die for democracy. It took me forever to solo, and then I ground-looped the primary trainer—a PT-17 Stearman biplane with open cockpit and goggles and helmet and a white silk scarf—twice. Once would have been enough to wash you out in peacetime, but the instructors just winced and smiled and told me practice makes perfect.

I went on to basic training in BT-13 Vultees, low-wing monoplanes with fixed landing gear. I knew the plane because we had kept one at the primary school to fly VD patients to an army hospital a few miles away. It was known as the Clapper Clipper. I distinguished myself in the Vultee by getting sick on fumes while learning acrobatics, and chucking up in the cockpit.

Advanced training was in AT-6s, that beautiful little plane by North American that was actually used as a combat aircraft in some countries—Kuwait and like that. I ground-looped that one, too. But Uncle Sam needed me, and those nice instructors kept on passing me through with fixed smiles, and before I knew it I was graduating with a couple of hundred other examples of the cream of America's youth, plus some RAF cadets who were a great bunch and who really did whistle little march tunes when they stepped off to a formation, just the way the prisoners did in *The Bridge Over the River Kwai.*

Getting our wings was a big deal. This was the time, according to all those Van Johnson movies, when Priscilla Lane showed up in white gloves and broad-brimmed hat and smelling of Chanel No. 5, and pinned them on your khaki shirt and stood on tippy toes to give you a big kiss with dark red passionate lips.

Since most of my class came from places like West Philadelphia or Sioux City, damn few sweethearts made it down to Selma, Alabama, to do the Priscilla Lane thing. We listened to a short speech by a general—someone had to give a speech twelve times a year at every advanced training base in the country; no wonder it was short—and pinned the wings on each other.

A few days later the orders were posted that would tell us what duty we were assigned to. No one cared very much where he was to be sent, but rather what he was to fly.

Since a lot of these stories are about a P-39, I'd better point out a few things that may sound technical at first, but I assure you are not. Every fighter plane had certain foibles. The P-40 had narrow landing gear which gave her a tendency to ground-loop if you let her swing the least bit on landing. Or even on takeoff. I remember a story an Australian flyer told me about the first P-40 squadron to arrive at Darwin in the early days of the war. They came in from the Philippines and Java, and everyone at the RAAF station watched these Yanks as they took care of their strange, aggressive-looking aircraft. And then the squadron leader started to take off, and halfway down the runway the P-40 ground-looped. She spun around in a cloud of red dust, and one wheel crumpled, and she caught a wing and cartwheeled, and in a second there was nothing left of her but a heap of twisted metal ticking quietly in the heat.

All the Aussies ran over, aghast, and the pilot miraculously crawled out of the wreckage and strolled away. And my friend ran up to him and said, "My God, what *happened?*"

And the Yank said, "Nothin' happened, son. She jest swung a little."

The P-38 had twin booms, each ending in an engine nacelle. She was very new to us, back then, and we all heard the stories about bailing out of her. You simply dropped between the booms. But if you didn't do it just right, the tail would slice you in two as cleanly as a sharp knife. That's what everyone said.

The P-39 had more than her share of bad habits. She had a rather sophisticated electrical system which took over jobs that the hydraulic system did on most planes. If you wanted to raise or lower the wheels, you just snapped a toggle switch on the dashboard, and there was a little whirring sound, and up or down they went. The same for flaps. The two switches were right next to each other, and the landing gear switch had a Plexiglas guard that angled over it so you wouldn't hit it by accident on the ground. But I watched a 39 land once and finish her run, and then instead of the flaps coming up, back to normal, up came the gear, and she stopped very suddenly with two bent propeller blades and the voice of the pilot coming over an open microphone with quiet resignation: "Shee-it."

The 39 had an electric propeller, with a little motor that adjusted the pitch of the blades when you moved the control. It would run away, sometimes, the blades not biting any air and so going faster and faster while the plane moved slower and slower.

Anyway, people called the P-39 a flying battery. We also called her a flying coffin, but hell, we called all the planes that.

She had an in-line liquid-cooled engine made by Allison that developed 1,150 horsepower. This big twelve-cylinder engine was mounted behind the cockpit, so the drive shaft extended all the way into the nose and there was geared to the propeller shaft. This allowed a cannon to be fitted inside the propeller shaft. The muzzle stuck out from the spinner, and if you could point your machine at a target you could presumably clobber it. The cannon was originally a 37-millimeter antitank gun which fired rather slowly—*whump-whump-whump,* like that—and

since you were sitting on it in the little cockpit, your legs strad-
dling it, the firing of it vibrated your prostate so that the whole
essence of war became mildly sexual. I do not know if this was
intentional.

Later cannon were 20-millimeter and fired much faster—
bababababababa, like that—and titillated you in a subtly different
way. Some men enjoyed it more. I was a 37-millimeter man
myself.

Beside the cannon were two .50-caliber machine guns syn-
chronized to fire through the propeller in the good old-fashioned
way; and out on the wings were four little .30-caliber machine
guns, which were later replaced by two .50s. When you flipped
on all three gun switches and fired your entire arsenal, there was
a great roaring noise—*braaaaap*—and the cockpit filled with
smoke so your eyes ran, and your airspeed dropped off a little.
All this weight of armament tended to compensate for the
engine being mounted amidships. But after you'd spent some
ammunition the center of gravity would slide back, and the
plane could do some strange things. It could tumble, for example. That means somersault, nose and tail swapping places as
it drops out of the sky. No plane ought to do that.

I did it once, practicing acrobatics in Florida. I was on my
back (". . . and there I was on my back with nothing on but
the radio . . ."—flyers' joke back then) and managed to stall
out, and she tumbled once, the sun swinging down past the
nose, and then the earth, while we fell 12,000 feet. Absolutely
terrifying.

But that wasn't the thing that was really wrong about the P-
39. The plane was simply underpowered for the kind of work it
was supposed to do. It could not climb high enough or quickly
enough, it could not go fast enough except in a dive (when it
had a tendency to go *too* fast), it could not maneuver handily

enough. Its controls were extremely delicate. The slightest hint of abruptness on the pilot's part would be rewarded with a high-speed stall, in which the lifting surfaces are "burbled" and suddenly fail to lift on one side. Result: a snap roll, which is a violent thing to do when you mean to and a real buster when you don't.

I had mixed feelings when I read the posted orders and found my name down for a P-39 operational training unit in Florida. Someone said "Park, you poor luckless bastard." And I said "What did you draw?" And he said "P-40s." And I said "Ground-looping son of a bitch." And he said "At least it don't tumble."

I bought a secondhand Ford convertible with another guy, both of us blowing our first pay as lieutenants. It was cheap, but it held together fine to get us down to Sarasota and fool around with down there. When I got shipped out, the other guy sold it. He never sent me my share because he got killed.

The drive down through Florida was fun because in those gas-rationed days we had the road to ourselves. It was dead straight, with only two lanes, like most roads back then, and knifed right through the swamps, black and fast, with bright green walls of foliage on each side.

We drove and dozed and looked for snakes crossing and harmonized on barbershop songs, which were for us what you would call campy. We sang a lot in those days. When I was a draftee in the Corps of Engineers we would march out to training problems singing "You Are My Sunshine." And when I was an aviation cadet we would march to formations singing "I've Got Sixpence," or even the Air Corps song, for God's sake. One terrible training officer would rack us back all the time and would sprint, red-faced and furious, up and down the length of our column as we marched off to the mess hall.

"Sing, Goddamn you!" he would screech, dancing with rage. I hope the bastard died.

Well, we ended up in Sarasota, winter home of the Ringling Brothers Barnum & Bailey Circus and the Boston Red Sox. The base was pleasantly shaded, with a fine long strip with the 39s parked near one end. One of the first people I met was a pilot who had graduated one class ahead of me and had been my own special upperclassman. We had a bit of hazing in those days— silly things like having an air raid, which meant crawling between the mattress and the springs of your bunk while the lights were out and then having any protruding parts of your body belabored when the lights were switched on again. But first, of course, the upperclassmen who were doing this had to ask permission: "May I touch you, mister?"

And if you laughed at all this nonsense, you had to wipe off your smile and throw it on the ground and stamp on it and get on your knees and bark at it.

This guy was sort of pleasant about the whole thing. He would come up to me while we were standing at stiff attention at five o'clock reveille and peer at me and say, "Ah there, Park, how is your libido this morning?" Whenever he hazed he did it in a nice way as if to say, "Look, this is a lot of crap, but I'm supposed to do it."

Anyway, those days were gone forever, and he was cordial and showed me my quarters and drove me down to the flight line in a jeep. He introduced me to some pilots in the ready room and gave me a sheaf of tech orders about the P-39 to go through. I had barely started on them when he returned and said, "Let's go look at a plane so you can get the feel of things while you're reading."

Perfectly reasonable. He led me out to this sleek, gleaming

creature, poised elegantly on her tricycle gear. She was dark green with a pale gray underbody, and her little door was open and a parachute in place on her bucket seat, its straps draped negligently over the back rest. I stepped up on the wing and carefully inserted myself in the cockpit—a tight fit. My mentor stood on the wing and saw me settled. "You can practice your cockpit check while you go on reading," he said. Of course.

He left, and I sniffed the cockpit scent of high-octane gasoline, old sweat, engine detergent, and just a hint of vomit, and ran through the cockpit procedure, running my hand from the knurled trim-tab controls up to the throttle quadrant and on to those famous electrical switches and then across the dashboard to touch and set the gyros and altimeter and remind myself where the other flight and engine instruments were. I did it about twice, and then there was my friend back again, looking down in on me from the wing.

"Think you know how to start her?"

"I doubt it."

"Try it," he said.

I dutifully switched on and pushed the prime pump a few times and rolled my heel on to the energizer. The sound moved gradually up the scale, higher and higher as the flywheel turned faster and faster. When the pitch leveled out at top speed I rolled my foot forward so my toe depressed the engager. The scream of the starter wheel abruptly wound down as the big propeller creaked around, jerkily, then faster when the first explosions shoved it. I pumped in another shot of prime, and the explosions erupted into galloping thunder. The plane shook savagely. The whole cockpit rattled, and dust flew from the seams.

My tutor leaned into the cockpit, the slipstream tugging at his shirt and pants. "Fine. Taxi down to the end of Number Three and wait for a green light from the tower. You've got a good forty-five minutes before operations closes down this afternoon.''

"Jesus," I shouted above the engine noise. "I don't—''

"Just piddle around, and it'll come to you.'' He waved airily and jumped off the wing.

I strapped up and released the brakes. The little plane almost leapt forward, coughing and barking like a hound at the sight of a shotgun. The radio crackled in my earphones, telling me to get down to the end of Number Three runway fast before my engine overheated. I hoped that it would.

The plane moved like a race car on the ground. I got to the appointed spot and ran the engine up to check the magnetos and pitch control. With a bit of throttle the galloping and vibration smoothed out to a lovely snarl, and the plane simply quivered against her brakes, her short, tapered wings glinting in the Florida sun. God, she was beautiful.

The green light blinked at me, meaning get going. I straightened up on the strip and locked my Sutton harness so I couldn't move anything but my arms and legs. Then I poured on the coal.

How to describe the first bedding of this strumpet? It was an exercise in sheer savagery, and I was never once in charge. Fortunately I had sense enough to adjust the trim tabs for torque. Otherwise, with that great propeller winding up to about 3,000 rpm, the slender little frame would have writhed over until it was going down the runway on two wheels and a wing tip. The tech orders had suggested getting the nose wheel up early on the takeoff run in order to save wear on the tire. So when I thought I was going fast enough to lift the nose I eased back very gently and *zam*—there we were at 500 feet.

Somehow I blundered out of the traffic pattern and got over

the beach at about 3,000 feet. Now for a couple of steep turns. I pressed stick and rudder firmly to the left, and *kaflump*—instant snap roll. Jesus Christ. I tried it to the right, very tenderly, and she made it, but quivering on the bitter edge of another high-speed stall all the while.

The only way to make a turn was to think about it. Think left, and around she'd go, nice as pie. Think steep turn, and she'd rack around so tightly that your eyeballs would sag.

The prospect of landing my violent partner—always a sort of climax which plane and pilot hopefully achieve together—rose momentarily to haunt me, but I put it off, resolving to learn first all I could of this strange and perilous body. We swung over the gulf, climbed to the puffy summer clouds, wound between a few with tender turns and gentle banks and then tried, very gingerly, a stall. Her nose rose and her speed fell and then I felt a tiny flickering in the palm of my hand, transmitted to me by the control stick. I had a sudden premonition of a reaction building up in her so unutterably rebellious that it didn't bear thinking about. "OK, OK," I muttered to her, and let her drop her nose and regain her speed. I simply lacked the courage to see what she would have done to me had I held her in a position which she so abominated.

With her nose below the horizon and her speed winding up, with her engine whining comfortably and her movements more docile—if more abrupt than I had ever known—I decided to land her. We howled over the field in a wide diving turn and I met the traffic pattern, trying frantically to slow down and at the same time hold our altitude. Then as we turned onto base leg I suddenly felt *too* slow and cracked on throttle to get the mushiness out of her. And then at last we were on approach, the flaps down, the wheels stiffly extended, vibrating against the slipstream, the runway coming up to meet us.

Nose up. Up more. Hold her. Straighten her quickly. Damn. We were down, more or less crookedly, the plane straightening herself out with the caster effect of her tricycle gear. A poor landing—the sort of effort you would expect from a virginal stranger to the bordello—but at least a safe one. She seemed merely contemptuous of me, not angry. I eased myself out of the cockpit, emotionally spent, drenched with sweat, trembling.

II

The Brotherhood

According to the movies, most of the flyers of World War II came from Texas. Oddly enough, most of the ones I worked with seemed to come from Iowa, where they had graduated from small colleges that were rather strong on the humanities. They had been the sort of boys who liked to fiddle with automobile engines in their spare time. Some had come from quite wealthy families. They were equally distributed between the political left and right, which in those days meant they were either for or against labor unions. We seldom argued about Roosevelt because we wanted to get the war over with and we felt he worked well with Churchill. We did argue about John L. Lewis.

If we had any things in common, they were physique and sexuality. As fighter pilots we were all five feet ten or less and all 160 pounds or less. Also we were well coordinated—some guys had been school or college athletes of some note. And the primitive psychiatric examinations that the army had given us ("Do you ever have wet dreams?") had either screened out the fags or badly discouraged them.

I remember one Texan—a short, blond man named Carter at Sarasota. I don't remember much about him except that for a Texan he was surprisingly quiet. I'm afraid he was quiet because he was stupid.

One morning some of us were sitting in the pilot's tent, watching John, our pet raccoon, drink a Coke. John would hang around the Coke machine until someone took pity on him and bought him a bottle and took the cap off for him. All you had to do then was hand it to him. John would hold it to his mouth and roll happily back on his spine to polish it off.

Quite abruptly we heard an engine sound, so different from the usual reduction-gear whine of the P-39 that we ducked outside to look. This was a high-pitched, tortured sound, a scream of mechanical pain still rising up the scale in its growing agony. It came from a 39 flying over the field with nightmarish slowness. The sight and sound affronted all we knew—a shriek of far-too-high engine revolutions coming from a plane moving far too slowly.

Someone shouted, "Runaway prop!" and then, "Who is it?"

Someone answered, "Carter." And then, "Jump, you dumb son of a bitch!"

Carter's electrical system had failed. The electrical control of his propeller blades had stopped working. Thus the blades had lost their pitch—the angle that gives them a bite of the air as they cut through it. They had flattened and were simply slicing through the air, faster and faster, meeting no resistance. They must have been forcing the engine speed up to twice its normal maximum of 3,000 rpms. But of course all that engine speed failed to move the plane because the propeller couldn't do its job. So there he was.

Carter had, in theory, certain things he could do to save himself. He had a manual control of his propeller pitch which would have given him a chance to get moving again—if he could make it cut in. But first he would have to reduce that engine speed, and at the same time keep flying. That meant he would have to lower the nose and let his ship dive for a moment. He had only 1,200 feet, however, not enough room to pick up much flying speed.

As we sorted out all these elements of his situation, we all started shouting, "Bail out! Bail out!" as though he could hear us. But poor Carter was facing something we couldn't know about. He never made the move.

We watched that terrible, screaming plane creep beyond the boundary of the field. Then there was a puff of smoke, very white against the warm blue sky. I suppose it was the engine coolant finally catching fire. The dying plane rolled lazily on its back and its nose dropped and it dove, first partly inverted and then simply straight down, making a vertical line toward the flat green earth as though it were hurrying to meet it the quickest way and get it over with. And it met the earth with a bright orange mushroom of flame, and for an awful second its scream kept reaching us, incongruously, while our eyes saw the cutting off of sound and life.

Then the scream stopped with a mild little *whump,* and the

flame turned to black smoke reaching quietly up, higher than Carter had been a few seconds before.

It was easy for us to see what Carter had done that was wrong. As long as we could distinguish the mistakes and picture ourselves handling an emergency in the right way, we could rebuild our confidence after a crash. So after I watched Carter "buy the farm" I would often wake up at night and think about it, and I would feel my muscles make the right moves—chop the throttle, nose down, now try the manual pitch control, ease on throttle, call the tower, and head in for an emergency landing. Or simply chop the throttle, nose down, manual control— no use, so quickly pull the red handle; feel the door fly off; snap open the Sutton harness and roll onto the wing, left shoulder touching it, right hand on the D-ring of the rip cord; pull quickly—and there you are. And off I'd go to sleep again.

Guppy was very annoying about *his* crash. Guppy was an Ivy Leaguer from Connecticut with black eyes and a perpetual expression of joyous surprise. Life was generally good to Guppy, and Guppy liked it that way.

One afternoon he brought a 39 in on one wing tip and rolled it into a tight little ball and walked out of the cockpit with a cheerful insouciance as if to say, "Doesn't *everybody* land like that?" Steve and I were down at the Lido—the beach was practically deserted at that time of year, October—and we heard the news from some other pilots and knew Guppy would show up to be entertaining about it. And he did and was. But we couldn't get out of him what had gone wrong.

"Come on, Guppy, what did you do, really, hit prop wash?"

"Look, I don't know. There wasn't another plane on the runway."

"But you can't just stub a wing tip for no reason."

"Watch me next time."

Steve was another easterner with a very solid New England concept of paying full measure for what he got out of life. He was upset because our flying schedule gave us too much time off. We would fly Monday afternoon and Tuesday morning, then be off duty from Tuesday noon until Thursday noon, and so on. We would head for the beach and swim and loll around and drink in the Lido up until Wednesday night so we could have Thursday morning to have hangovers. Steve would fret ıbout it and say we weren't learning enough.

"What do you want to be, the scourge of the skies?" Guppy would ask him.

"I want to be able to do what I'm told and live."

"Why not just pretend to do what you're told?"

"That sort of thing catches up to you," Steve would say, ominously.

Steve really believed in duty, honor, country, and also, perhaps incongruously, in human decency. He saw the best in his fellows and tried to fit himself among them. He was a very good man and he eventually became my squadron commander.

To all three of us, the war was something that should unquestionably be fought. We were only concerned with how best to get it over with and survive. And we were all aware that the method we had stumbled into—being fighter pilots for the army—was not a particularly safe way of life.

Guppy had joined this branch because his father had flown in World War I. Steve had been an ROTC graduate and had transferred to the cadets after Pearl Harbor because this seemed to him the right thing to do. I had been a draftee in the Corps of Engineers for six months before Pearl Harbor. I didn't mind it, but after watching four P-40s land at old Bolling Field in Washington, D.C. (one of them ground-looped, incidentally) and four dapper young men get into a commmand car and go roaring off to the officers' club to get plastered, I decided that life was for me. I got my transfer just *before* Pearl Harbor and my first reaction upon hearing the news of the attack that Sunday afternoon was to wonder if there was a way to rethink my decision. However, my cowardice was matched only by my inertia, so I drifted along toward what I considered inevitable early death.

There were many pilots I knew who honestly loved what they were doing, who could not rest easy until they felt they had flailed the skies and loosed a hail of bullets at every enemy plane that ever flew. They would complain when they had a day off; they would moan when their mission did not invite combat. I knew these young men and some of them I quite liked. But I never fully understood them.

There were others who were devoted to the whole exercise of flight to the exclusion of everything else. They tended to abhor combat because it might be injurious to their planes, but they would accept it as a technological plateau that their machines were built to achieve. They could talk about nothing but aviation; they were doing what they loved and knew best though admittedly not the way they'd like to do it.

Most of the men I knew and worked with were civilian groundlings at heart who had joined up quite simply to fight for their country, whatever that meant, and went bouncing through this strange and savage environment with varying degrees of tolerance and endurance. Some found themselves while flying fast little aircraft and firing guns. Some were sent home for psychiatric treatment. Some were naturally good at it, but hated it; some were naturally poor at it, but loved it.

Steve was quite good at the job because he worked at it. He also had a dimension of responsibility that fitted him for command. Guppy was *very* good at the job (he became an ace) despite the fact that he despised every minute of it and plotted incessantly to find a way safely out. I was quite poor at it most of the time and more or·less resigned to being marked for destruction. But I was saved by a breathtakingly lovely brown-green-gray Airacobra with a delicious smell all her own who accepted me with resignation and then, incredibly, with a stirring of her pure metallic soul that can only be called a kind of love. She saved me again and again, and she nurtured me and equipped me, at least for survival.

Yes. Nanette. I still remember you, Nanette.

The Winter of '42

In order to meet my mistress I traveled a long road. We were a depression generation, unused to travel. But now we savored portions of life that were never designed for young men fresh out of college during the Depression. Three Pullmans took us from Florida to New Orleans to Los Angeles to San Francisco, and we lived in compartments and ate that extraordinary dining-car food served by competent, ever-grinning Uncle Toms.

We watched the land as it was then roll by our windows: the

endlessly untouched red-dirt South; the French Quarter of New Orleans with lacy ironwork and the smell of flowers and incredible cooking, and hardly a sign, then, to tell you you were there; the Texas plains going on forever, and a real cowboy on a real horse galloping along beside the train for a moment and then veering off with a wave; the Rockies; Hollywood, and a night club where Bette Davis came in and where everyone was nice to us because we were in uniform and were obviously on our way to kill those rotten yellow-bellied little Japs and thus preserve democracy in this great land of ours; the spectacular journey up through the mountains to San Francisco—one marvelous view after another, marred only by passing very slowly a train full of those rotten yellow-bellied little Japs, only these were Nisei, worried-looking truck gardeners and their wives and solemn children, all waving little American flags at us as they headed for a concentration camp. The sight disturbed us for a moment, but we were due in San Francisco in half an hour, so we shrugged it off.

Finally we were crammed aboard a Norwegian freighter, 300 pilots and 300 ground crew jammed into the holds in five tiers of bunks, the latrines awash with vomit, the meals cut to two a day, both times frankfurters turning green with mold. And in the cabin quarters, up adjoining the bridge, some two dozen army ground officers with their bright little badges proclaiming that they belonged to the coast artillery or cavalry for God's sake, slept in staterooms and ate steaks. They didn't outrank us. Most of them were lieutenants like us. But you see they were real army men, not just amateurs who were not fit to wear the uniform and were only allowed in this glorious war because someone had to do things like fly airplanes. So they ate their steak dinners and leaned on the after-rail of their superstructure, looking down with faint amusement at the rest of us, swarming around the waist of the ship, lining up endlessly for those two revolting meals. Oh, I won't forget you, you starched bastards.

Townsville. A small sugar-cane port on the coast of tropical Queensland. It was jammed to the sewers with troops—huge Australians in their broad-brimmed hats and their jungle-green shirts, British and Dutch naval officers in spotless white shorts, American airmen in sloppy, uncreased khaki. We found that on the Esplanade, a palm-shaded boulevard beside the harbor, one fine old mansion housed the American Army Officers Club. So, innocently, we went around there, a dozen of us, to get a meal. We could smell the steaks and chops cooking as a captain in bright cavalry boots and Sam Browne belt opened the door. "I'm sorry," he said stiffly. "Air Corps people are not admitted. Ground officers only." And the door closed. Prick.

Charters Towers. An all-day train trip on the sugar-cane line to get eighty miles inland where gold miners had settled "The Towers" a generation ago. A nice countryside where rolling grassy hills were spotted with gum trees at such regular intervals they seemed to have been planted. Yet it was wild rangeland, with kangaroos bounding off incredibly outside our camp and a koala bear that allowed itself to be adopted by one tent. It slept in a flying boot and would scrabble across the tent floor every morning to greet us all as we passed on the way to breakfast.

The camp was lovely, but the water was bad and the doctor was hopelessly alcoholic. We all got dysentery. I remember those long lines of drooping, half-naked men waiting outside the stinking latrines in that softly beautiful countryside.

Steve and Guppy and I used to play cards a lot while we were recovering. There was a game called rat fink that we enjoyed. Then we began to get hungry—hungrier even than we had been on that troopship. We learned that there was a Red Cross servicemen's club about ten miles from the base where they served real food. One of the mechanics told us about it.

When we felt well enough, we hitched a ride on a truck and arrived with the smell of cooking deliriously near. We jumped off the truck and, bright-eyed and slavering, headed for the dining room. Lots of people were there, eating things like baked ham and macaroni and cheese, veal Parmesan, meat loaf, homemade lasagna, lima beans running with butter, hot biscuits, and honey. We were dancing with hunger.

And this perfectly beautiful American girl came over to us. She was tall and chic in her Red Cross uniform, marvelously built, clear-skinned and shiny-haired, looking at us with wide-spaced dark eyes, softly luminous.

"You can't come in here," she said. "This is for enlisted men only. Officers aren't allowed."

We did a little flying, at last, at Charters Towers. The planes had been in combat squadrons in New Guinea. They were battle-weary and had been sent down south to die; some had bullet holes covered over with Band-Aids. I stalled one into a snap roll while I was trying to loop it—a wonderful evasive maneuver except that the whole canopy sprang loose, and a great tornado of wind howled into the cockpit and picked up all the dust under my feet—chewing-gum wrappers and dried sputum and cigar ash—and blew it into my eyes.

Three guys were killed on those planes. One was a red-neck from Alabama who managed to get drunk every night and then wake up everybody in all the tents by bragging about the poontang he'd latched onto in the village, going on endlessly and loudly about how he had the biggest prick in northern Australia, and how she came six times to his one. And everyone would groan and snarl in all the other tents and tell him that he *was* the biggest prick in northern Australia, and one night

Steve—nice, peaceable Steve—fished out his big Colt pistol and told him that if he didn't shut the hell up he was going to die.

And then, not long after, he made a nose-high turn from base leg onto final approach and the plane slid out from under him and dumped into the trees 300 feet below. When people got to him they found that one leg had been severed at the hip, and he had bled to death.

Conners had to bail out when a plane he was flying simply quit working. He landed in a lonely stretch of country, but near a road, and he saw two little kids running toward him. They were on their way home from school, and this was obviously the biggest day in their whole lives—a Yank pilot dragging about four miles of parachute behind him and asking them if they could lead him to a telephone.

They took him back to their homestead and he called the base and pretty soon a truck came out to pick him up. Connors wanted to give the kids a present, so he searched through his escape kit—the little packet that was attached to the back of his parachute seat. He didn't think a pistol was a very good idea, and certainly not an injection vial of morphine. But there was this bar of iron-ration chocolate—twenty small squares, so packed with nutrients that each one was to serve as a complete meal. He cracked it in two for the kids and explained that it was a different kind of chocolate and you had to go very easy on it. But as the truck drove away, and he looked back to wave, he saw that they'd already gone from Monday breakfast to Wednesday lunch.

Charters Towers back to Townsville. And there we had an air raid. Sirens went off one evening, and searchlights went on, and everyone piled outside—we were in barracks beside the airfield—and peered up at a tiny moving spot of light in the night sky. We never found out what it was, whether, in fact, it was a Japanese plane or a lost and wandering ally. Not a shot was fired at it; not a bomb was dropped from it.

Finally, Townsville to Port Moresby, New Guinea. We crawled into a small fleet of B-17 bombers to make the flight, and I can remember, when we crawled out of them again, how the heat thumped us on the back of the head like a soft mallet.

All impressions of New Guinea are extreme—the heat solid and palpable, the smells rich enough to grow crops, the colors so sharp and pure they make your eyes wince. The sun has an undiffused brilliance and when it touches something green, like a leaf, it isn't your everyday humdrum leaf-green. It's nature's finest Goddamn green and it socks you right in the eyeball. The same with blue sky and black forest-tree trunks and red soil and white cumulus clouds and cobalt blue water and the red sun rising. The colors are so intense they make you visually drunk.

Away from the business of the airstrip, I could see a tumbling blue line of mountains on the horizon. They were the kind of mountains a five-year-old kid paints to get rid of his phobias—impossible overhangs, saw teeth that lacked all order, peaks that rose ridiculously like admonitory fingers, needles, spikes, cliff walls straight out of Hollywood ("Me no go there, Bwana, that Tarzan country!").

I was still agape when a jeep appeared with a dusty youth with dusty chevrons who read some names. Four of us piled aboard with our gear. Steve and I and two others. Guppy was whisked off somewhere else. We bounced along a dirt track and came to a hillside, and there we were shown a scattering of green four-man tents. In one of them Steve and I dumped our barracks bags and claimed two empty cots. Then we were driven down the hill to an airstrip made of steel matting and beside it an open-walled, grass-thatched house. And we walked in and found sixteen men staring at us.

To someone used to so many months of careful army indoctrination and formality, these specimens seemed nearly naked. Most wore khaki shorts made by knifing off the legs of issue pants. Some had flying suits—one-piece coveralls—pulled loosely on over the shorts and left unzipped to the waist. One wore a T-shirt with "Purdue AA" on it. Many wore fleece-lined flying boots that had never been American issue. I soon learned that you could get them from the Australian flyers in a swap for a Colt .45 automatic, plus a bottle of our squadron whiskey.

My new colleagues were sitting or lying on a cluster of army cots that almost filled the floor of the hut. Groups were quietly playing bridge; loners were dealing out hands of solitaire or reading tarnished paperbacks. One quartet was playing Monopoly. They were all painfully thin and rather ivory-colored. They gleamed with stale sweat. Their hair was cut so short it seemed to have been razored off. Many men wore mustaches, some quite big. No one wore any kind of badge or sign of rank.

I was nudged toward a tall, thin man with a drooping mustache who was wiping the back of his neck with a dark green Australian army shirt. I went up to him firmly and saluted. "Lieutenant Park reporting, sir."

Someone on a nearby cot dropped his cards and said "Oh, Christ," quietly. The commanding officer put down his shirt and looked at me in mild surprise as I held my salute. "Forget that shit," he said.

He shook hands and introduced me around. I met Airedale and Termite and Python and Piss-Ant and so on through an astonishing lexicon, mostly of natural history. It seemed that almost everyone in my squadron was some sort of animal. Another thing I noticed was that they all sharpened their sheath knives incessantly. They all seemed to have little carborundum stones, and whenever there was a pause in conversation, a delay in dealing a hand, any hiatus of any kind, out would come the stones and the blades and there would be this moody rasp and stroke, eyes focused on distant space. They would test their blades on the hair of their forearms, shaving patches of it off. You could tell the guys in my squadron anywhere by the baldness of their forearms.

The pilots said hello to me and to the other replacements with grave courtesy and half-concealed stares of appraisal. They were surprisingly solicitous about our comfort, the attendance upon our needs. After we had been in the squadron for a while we came to realize that this kindness toward new members developed partly because these were normally quite pleasant young men who every day were getting rid of whatever tensions might have made them short-tempered and selfish; and also they saw in every new face a possible ticket home. No one could be rotated back to the States until a replacement had showed up—and managed to stay alive long enough to become a real member of the family.

The commanding officer, a major named Jim, suggested that we get into something comfortable and take an orientation flight. Thus three of us joined an old pilot named Skunk-Ass and went out to meet the planes. I had been used to the junk we had flown at Charters Towers and had forgotten the delight of well-loved, well-maintained P-39s. This was a line squadron—no transient outfit—and it had twenty-six planes, out of which it had to keep sixteen in the air. There were plenty of top-notch air mechanics to maintain a mere ten aircraft, operating on them, sewing them up again, dieting them, giving them proper rest, washing them, and caressing them.

They all looked perfectly beautiful, these 39s, their sleekly nubile little bodies waxed, their guns armed and taped over the muzzles to keep out rust, their engines constantly warm. Most were dark green on top and gray-blue on their bellies. Often one wore a camouflage of browns and yellows. Every nose cone was painted buff, so also the top of each fin and rudder: That was our squadron color. On each rudder and nose was the squadron number—in the 70s or 170s for Red Flight, 80s or 180s for Blue Flight, and other similar sequences for Yellow and White.

Many doors or noses carried the names of the pilot and crew chief and sometimes a brightly painted cartoon figure or animal which illustrated the plane's name: Honey Bee, Macushla, Stinger, Tovarich, Li'l Devil, Panther, Elaine B., and so on. Some planes carried small Japanese flags painted beside the pilot's name—his victories. It was apparent that not only could a man aspire to having his own ship, he might actually do something violent and effective with it.

Under each wing a crew chief dozed in the shade. As our jeep approached a revetment, he would leap up and stand beside the right wing, above which was the cockpit door. When I debarked beside a D-model P-39, a mahogany-tanned figure in greasy shorts was there to help me into the cockpit and strap me into place with the same care that a small boy gets when he is buttoned up to go out and play in the snow. He looked in on me with beaming encouragement as I energized and engaged the engine. Then with a pat on my canopy he was gone, and I was rolling out of the revetment and falling into line behind one of the others.

Skunk-Ass had told us that we would take off in pairs. We

hadn't done this since flying school, and then not often since safety regulations were intensely enforced in the States. But here in a combat zone there was no nonsense about endangering innocent civilians, so we made up our own rules. To take off, we tucked the wing of the second plane inside that of the first, just back of its tail. The pilot of the second plane simply watched his leader and when he saw the first plane leave the ground he knew that he had left it too. When he saw his leader's wheels retract, he snapped his own switch.

Thus the first element—two planes—broke from the runway and began a gentle turn. And the second element, which had started down the runway as the first passed the halfway mark, rose after it and turned inside it. And by the time 180 degrees of turn had been accomplished, the second element had caught up with the first and was securely in formation. The flight—four planes—then consisted of flight leader and Number Two echeloned to the right, then the element leader (Number Three) and Tail-Ass Charlie (Number Four) echeloned to the left. Today they call this a finger-four formation because the planes take the position of your four fingertips when you spread them slightly. We had no name for it—it was just the combat formation developed by Chennault and his Flying Tigers so that everyone could see what was happening to everyone else. The second element would cross over behind the first more or less at will, and the planes within the elements would space themselves so they could see the whole sky and not run into each other. The flight would be joined by the other three flights that made up the squadron, and all four of them would weave gently back and forth at slightly different altitudes as they sailed off on their mission.

I can still feel that first indoctrination flight in New Guinea. It was late afternoon, and the slanting sunlight turned everything bright gold except the sea and the high sky directly overhead. The mountain range—the Owen Stanleys—was lost by now in a massive cumulus buildup, and the great clouds still creamed upward, gilt-edged and voluptuous. Over the sea the air was silk-smooth and so was the engine, and the four of us snarled along peacefully together, looking down at the bomb-shattered little town of Port Moresby.

We turned gently toward Kokoda Pass, where the Australians had trudged upward through endless muck and finally stopped the Japanese, who had been doing their trudging from the other direction. Both forces were exhausted and shot with malaria, but the Japanese supply line was stretched too far, and their soldiers couldn't overwhelm the Australians with numbers, which is about the only way anyone could beat Australian infantry. So the fighting tumbled back downhill from Kokoda and ended up around Buna on the north coast. And there the Australians cleaned up the Japanese attack on Moresby once and for all. There were some Americans there, too, learning how. And my squadron had been overhead.

We swung close to the cloud-sheathed mountains and then back down in a long, screaming slant above the quilt of rain forest until we popped across the coast again, very low, and aimed at the rusted prow of a sunken ship. "Thirties only," said Skunk-Ass's voice in my ears, and I switched on my gunsight and the toggle switch for the outside guns. Holding formation with one eye, I got the sight on the red iron blob and squeezed off. The wing guns rattled faintly in my ears, and I had the satisfaction of seeing a few tracers ricochet off the wreck.

We veered away and swung, still low, toward our strip. Skunk-Ass waggled his wings, and we obeyed the signal, tucking in close to him. "Echelon to the right," he said, and the second element swung under him and took a position beside and astern of the Number Two man. The planes were now forming a straight line, angled back and to the right of the leader. I was flying Number Two, my eyes now glued on Skunk-Ass, so near I could almost touch him. He had a buff-colored leather football helmet with a rim of sponge rubber around it. His oxygen mask flapped under his chin as he turned his head to check position.

Then his plane began to drop beside me, and I kept with him, slanting toward the end of the strip, picking up speed. At about fifty feet we shot down the length of the strip, and then, suddenly Skunk-Ass was gone, jerked upward and to the left so abruptly that his wing tips carved smooth traceries of condensation in the hot air. I came back on my stick, pressing left and pushing the left rudder, and my cheeks sagged as I soared up and swung left, now well behind the leader. The others followed, and thus we were all four strung out on the downwind leg of the landing pattern, 600 feet high, moving slowly enough to snap down the wheels. I saw Skunk-Ass drop and turn toward the strip again—not the square-cornered turn we had been taught, but a steep, fluid curve all the 180 degrees from downwind to approach. Without being fully conscious of the landing pattern, I was following my leader right into the slot, and the strip of linked steel matting was now on my plane's nose, gleaming invitingly in the low sun. I snapped the flaps all the way down and slid nicely onto the metal with a little squeal of rubber, and the mats undulated and rattled under me as I slowed.

One by one we taxied toward the revetments past a tall, thin figure mopping himself with a green shirt. Jim, the CO, was finding out what kind of pilots he had drawn. As we came back to the alert shack, our flying suits unzipped and flapping about us, dark with sweat, he drew the three of us replacements together.

"That was kind of pisspoor," he said. I was rather hurt. It was the best landing I'd made for weeks. "The idea is to get all the ships on the ground as fast as possible so our friends"—Jim nodded toward the mountains; he always called them "our friends"—"can't catch us with wheels down in the traffic pattern. Next time, stack your echelon *above* your lead ship when you buzz the strip." He showed us with his hands. "That way the flight leader can get as low as he wants without wiping someone out. Shit, Skunk-Ass had to keep about thirty feet high with you guys stacked *below* him, and then you ended up spread all over the sky instead of peeling up tight. Watch the last flight land when they come in. Pretty soon now."

We reentered the alert shack, subdued. No one looked up from the solitaire hands, the bridge game, the endless Monopoly, played with humorless intensity. I wandered over to the operations desk—an island in the middle of the cots—where there were two field telephones in leather boxes. There were papers on the metal top and a stack of blue-bound notebooks. A blackboard stood beside the desk: on one side four columns labeled Red, Blue, Yellow, and White, and four names under each—last names, like Briscoe and Petersen and Wheeler and Niemo and Millet and Gray and Fennaut and Fishbein.

On the other side of the blackboard was written, in capitals, "JAPANESE AIR STRENGTH," and under that were listed New Guinea bases—Lae, Salamaua, Madang, Finschafen, Wewak, Hollandia, and several more—each with the fighters and bombers believed to be based there. The total came to something like 800. I didn't know what our strength was, but I knew we only had three bases on New Guinea—Moresby, Milne Bay, and Dobodura (the airstrip for Buna). And I knew that I was right in the middle of a good part of the air strength for Moresby.

A pleasant-looking officer in khakis with a damp, red face and steaming spectacles came over and introduced himself. "I'm Elkhart, the intelligence officer," he said. "We're very glad to get you fellows. Hope everything's settling down all right. When you get a chance you should keep up to date on the blue books." He indicated the stack on the desk and handed me one. I opened it at random and was quickly entranced: "Diary of Ito Matsuko, Warrant Officer, Imperial Japanese Army, found at Dobodura" and "Test-flying the 'Oscar'-type fighter." The Oscar was a Japanese fighter that I knew was widely used in this area.

I started to read, but a voice called, "Here they come!" and I put it down and made for the outside. I found I was reacting with strangely nervous speed, and I realized why. The roomful of men, despite the desultory conversation and the lazy slap of cards, was jittering with tension. Every sudden sound, every raised voice, every ring of the phone produced instant silence, breathless waiting, an expectancy so infectious that I was already catching it on my first exposure as a member of the squadron.

Many of the old pilots went out with us replacements to see the last flight down. I looked around helplessly, and someone pointed toward the approach end of the strip, where faraway, low-down, and coming fast, I saw a bolt of angular metal, the sun glinting on its knobs and notches. It came at the strip too fast for its sound to warn of what was going to happen, and it came at us so low that I saw yellow dust swirl behind it, churned by the propellers. And then it smashed over our heads in a great wave of noise and power, four P-39s so tightly drawn together that they seemed one.

Violently, they broke the bolt apart, one after another sweeping upward and to the left, their wing tips creaming the air with condensation. They leapt upward and spread like the ribs of a fan. Each plane hung momentarily at the top of its climb, banking vertically for its turn into pattern, and at that moment the sleek underbodies cracked open and the landing gear unfolded, screaming protest against the slipstream. With mere seconds between them—perhaps 200 yards—they dropped back toward the end of the strip in a tight gliding turn with some slip in it. Flooded cylinders spluttered, air shrieked through the extended struts, flaps broke the contour of the wings as the planes slowed this chilling drop above the scrub trees. And at the last second the wings flicked horizontal, the noses reared up like drowning men gasping for air, the wheels reached for ·the runway and found it with a spurt of smoke and that click and rattle of the metal sheets. It seemed that all four were safely down before I could absorb what I was seeing.

We had moved down to the edge of the strip and so were close by when the four planes taxied back, their propellers windmilling aimlessly, their windows rolled down, and bare, sweat-shined elbows sticking out of them to catch the warm wind. All the violence had gone out of the machines. They were ungainly and spent.

A new N model led, olive paint waxed so it glistened, buff nose cone and fin tip freshly painted, the squadron number sharp and clear. Inside, a sallow, dark-eyed face under a ragged cloth helmet with a thick leather crash band around the circumference. The hairy hand on the window sill flicked up and down in greeting as the flight leader trundled past. Then came a bat-

tered P-400 (the export version of the P-39 which had been po-
litely and firmly rejected by the RAF earlier in the war) with a
long 20-millimeter cannon sticking out from the spinner. Its
brown-green camouflage had been flaked away to give an uncer-
tain impression of gray. Streaks of mud had spattered the underbody and been etched permanently in place by prop wash. Only
the windshield was clean, and behind was a pale young face
under a new helmet with amber goggles pushed to the crown. It
turned and smiled hesitantly at us, then snapped anxiously back
again, intent on guiding the machine. This had to be a relatively
new man—the nervousness and the Number Two position indicated it—and I realized that this was how I had looked earlier.

Number Three was a D-2 model with 37-millimeter cannon
and a gaudy Disneyish animal painted on the door. The name
Happy Tiger was splashed on the nose section in orange paint,
and under it, in clean stencils, "1st Lt. H. R. Chase" and under
that, "Crew Chief, S/Sgt. J. Potter." Behind the door were
three neatly painted Japanese flags.

The last ship was another N model, sleek and green, taxiing
far too fast. I caught a glimpse of the squadron number, 74, and
of a broad face under a maroon baseball cap: dark glasses; a
blond mustache; the gleam of teeth as the hand on the sill rose,
the middle finger flourished in vulgar greeting. Then a swirl of
slipstream enveloped me in dust, and I turned away with something in my eye. "That Goddamn Badger," someone said. "He
didn't want to fly Tail-ass Charlie so now he dusts us all off."

That evening I drank whiskey with these strange young men
up in the farmhouse—a small building atop a small hill in the
middle of our squadron tents. Some genius had built a simple
bar in it after the squadron adopted it, and there is nothing that
turns an abandoned and dilapidated shack into a pleasant and
hospitable clubroom faster than a bar. It had music—a wind-up

Victrola which someone lugged faithfully down to the alert shack every morning and back to the farmhouse every night. It had lights from a sputtering generator out on the dark hillside. It had a short-wave radio on which I heard that first night, for the first time, the softly American-girl's voice of Tokyo Rose introducing hits by Glenn Miller and Artie Shaw and warning specific squadrons and bomb groups of their impending doom. The whiskey was cheap and the cards slapped on the tables in serious poker and cigars wreathed smoke and one after another the drawn-faced, cordial pilots said hello and asked how things were in the States. And I kept wondering, as I met them and awkwardly used their animal names, what in the name of God I was doing here.

IV

Sloth and Cold Showers

I have always thought that the main reason I joined the Army Air Forces was that I was made to take cold showers in prep school. My father was a Boston minister among whose myriad duties was the "prep-school circuit" of New England, preaching on Sunday afternoons in one white cupolaed school chapel after another before pews full of dark-clad youths with varying degrees of acne and stiff white collars. They would all be remarkably silent, except for inevitable readjustments of mucus, while my father—or whoever it was—gave a thoughtful little sermon, and then they would erupt with thunderous volume into "Our God, Our Help in Ages Past."

Prep schools, then, became part of our family conversation. Not a big part, but enough so that we all expected to go to one. The tuition came from somewhere; I don't think it was very much in those Depression days. We all carefully chose different ones, and off we went at age fourteen.

I ended up in a Massachusetts school where the Puritan ethic was pounded into me: Dull sloth is the greatest of all sins, followed closely by cowardice, masturbation, smoking, dishonesty, and uncleanliness. A pealing bell in our white cupola woke us at quarter to seven, and we would slam our windows down against the biting cold and pad down the corridor to the huge tiled bathroom where three showers were running steadily—ice-cold. Off would come our pajamas, and, trying to conceal our youthful erections (now rapidly subsiding at the horrid prospect), into the shower we would go for a few gasping seconds. It was without any question the hardest thing I ever did in my life.

Of course it felt grand when it was over. We would dance out of the misery and rub ourselves down vigorously and snap our damp towels at each other's pink little rumps, and then, as another bell tolled, we would dash back to our rooms to dress in yesterday's underwear and socks and today's compulsory clean white shirt and this term's slightly undersized suit.

We attended strenuous classes in Latin and Algebra and French and American History and Physics and Music and Bible and English. We were swamped with assignments and spent at least three hours a day in supervised study hall where, if we giggled when someone noisily broke wind, we were sent to the room of an eighteen-year-old monitor who cracked us on the bare bottom with a paddle.

Every afternoon we flung ourselves into athletics with all the zeal that our vigorous young masters could summon within us. Football was compulsory. Team after team dotted the playing fields, ranging from the Pups, calling signals in treble voices, to the First Team, which was seldom scored on, much less lost a game.

I went into all this determined to do as well as my siblings, whom I considered—most unjustly, it turns out—to be achievers. I floundered as far as Cicero, destroyed the French language, shuddered to a bewildered halt in Algebra and was only saved by slipping gratefully into Geometry. I enjoyed football but was far too wispy to achieve glory and ended up with a badly broken left arm. When that happened I was allowed to do cross-country running, which was considered an activity suitable only for flits, which was our word for fags, fairies, finks, what-have-you. How much better it would have been, I would think, to play up, play up and play the game—and bust the other arm.

At morning assembly the headmaster, with his great tall forehead and his monumental assurance of what it took to become a New England gentleman, would speak directly at me about the joys of courage and honesty and scholastic success and cleanliness, and I would writhe with the full realization of my failures. Sloth? I was enslaved by sloth. I also was now an established flit; I was tormented by fantasies concerning one master's wife who filled a sweater like no one before—or since; I had sneaked a puff of a cigarette when forced to by a larger and braver lad; I lied when my cowardice made it essential. I was a disaster.

The only thing I did well was take a cold shower. That frightful little ritual took on a certain significance for me because it was obviously senseless and therefore *had* to fit the basic cultural ground rule that I was being taught: If you do something *hard,* everything will come out OK.

So here I was in a fighter squadron in New Guinea, about to go winging off on a career for which I was ill-trained and equipped and to which I was morally and viscerally opposed. If that wasn't the biggest Goddamn cold shower in the world it was at least the best I could do.

V

Initiation

Before that first evening in the squadron ended, there was a stir of activity around a bulletin board beside the bar. The operations sergeant had posted tomorrow's flight list, and we gathered to read it: two escort missions over the mountains to Wau, a gold-mining settlement in a hidden valley. Both missions were to escort transport planes—old Douglas C-47s—carrying infantry, since Wau was almost surrounded by Japanese who had wrenched themselves over the coastal ridges from their base at Salamaua. "The Nips want that gold," an old pilot explained. "So we carry the Aussies up there to stop them."

"Is there a strip there?"

"Yeah, sort of. Wait till you see it—it runs uphill, right into the side of a mountain. There's no going around to make another pass at it. Those bus drivers land uphill, turn around, hold their brakes on while the Aussies jump out, then rev up, release their brakes and roar right off, down the ski jump."

"And what do we do?"

"We circle around and wait so the Zeros won't bounce them. They never do come in to Wau though, until we're over the pass on the way home, without enough fuel to turn back."

"You mean they know when that is?"

"Shit! Those fuckers know everything. You'll see."

Two of us replacements were scheduled for weather flights preceding the escort missions. These were two-plane affairs to scout the weather over the target area and call it back before the flights took off. Radio communication from Wau didn't have the power to reach all the way to Moresby—and anyway, the Japs would surely be monitoring it. My name appeared on the morning weather hop, flying wing on Chase, whom I had watched land that afternoon and whose real name turned out to be Rabbit.

I slept fitfully, even though the cot had an air mattress, a luxury reserved for line squadrons. I was really ticking away at last—as is so often the case—when a persistent sound intruded: a voice in the darkness calling, "Early flights! Early flights!" and interspersing the cry with raucous turns of a watchman's rattle.

The weather hop was the earliest flight of all, so I fumbled into my flying suit by flashlight, trying not to wake up Steve and Lambert, who were not scheduled. Steve was awake anyway. "Have fun," he said, and I said I'd try.

Outside in the blackout I could only feel my way downhill toward the mess tent by the smell of coffee. The brightness inside was startling. A pudgy cook shoved a mug of coffee at me and indicated a line of stainless steel containers—cold cereal, powdered milk, thick, plate-sized pancakes, prunes lurking in a dark pool of juice, thick-cut bacon with the rind still on. I joined a couple of others of the first flight and picked my way past this array. Prunes and cereal roughage seemed the very last thing my digestive tract required. I tried a pancake, dabbing it with canned butter which tasted like candle wax and pouring over it some hot sweetened water. It was awful, but edible. The bacon was mostly uncooked fat and produced no joy. The coffee was old but hot. I took my mess to a long table, and Chase came to join me.

He briefed me quickly about what to expect: "A weather flight is like taking a day off. You just drive on up there and then turn back and drive home. You call in the weather by code as soon as you're over the range and can pick up radio contact with Wau."

"What's the code?"

"We'll see when we get to the alert tent. It changes all the time because the Nips can hear it, too."

"Does the squadron call sign change too?"

"Not often. We'd never be able to remember it. We've been Gopher for months and probably will stay that way. We all like it. The base name changes once in a while. It used to be Queenie before it was Mary."

Chase and I drove to the line in the operations jeep, along with the ops officer and his clerk, a sergeant from Louisiana who, someone told me later, had been going for a PhD when he had been drafted. We passed the revetments, which were glowing with eerie blue light from the exhausts of the planes being preflighted. The noise of the engines washed over us. I was assigned to Number 74, but didn't know in which revetment it was parked. Some of the engines sounded rough and cold, and I presumed, gloomily, that one of those would be 74.

Yet I hardly had time to be nervous, for Chase and I had to make our report before the transports were ready for takeoff, which would be little more than an hour away—soon after it was light enough to load them. We kept the jeep running while we helped the operations people draw tight the tent flaps and light the lamps. Weaver, the ops officer, went to the field phone, turned the crank and spoke, writing on a slip of paper. He returned to us.

"Charlotte is flyable; Lucy is closed in. OK?"

We nodded and picked out our Mae Wests from the orange line of them, hanging along one tent wall. I strapped mine on over my shoulder holster. I saw that Chase had his sheath knife tied outside the calf of his leg. That looked very tough, and I decided to do that later.

If there *was* a later, that is. I didn't really think I was going to buy the farm on this mission, but it seemed like bad luck to make any plans. After all, people had said that some frightening proportion of pilots were killed on their first missions, and here I was getting all trussed up for it, like a Long Island duckling in the slaughter room. "Let's go," said Chase, and we slipped through the tent and headed for the jeep.

We roared off to the revetments, and I had a sick feeling that I was headed for a night takeoff, which I had never done and had no desire to do in a P-39. But by the time I had jumped down beside Number 74 and been stuffed into the cockpit by the crew chief, there was a faint glow in the east. It was still too dark to see the face that went with these competent hands which were finding my parachute straps for me and setting the Sutton harness so that I would be pinned against the seat for takeoff, but when he moved off the wing with a pat on my shoulder and I looked up from the blue light of the cockpit where I had been tuning the radio, I found that there was a barely distinguishable aura of light. I could see the tapering nose of my plane, I could see the graceful wings. And, most important, I could make out a horizon.

I had my heel on the energizer, the whine building in my ears, when I heard the blast of an engine taking hold nearby and knew that Chase had started. I rolled my toes onto the engager, shot in a squirt of prime and with a little flash of flame from the exhaust stacks behind me, my engine came alive. Beautiful. Chase's plane rolled past my revetment, and the figure beside my right wing waved me forward. I released the brakes and trundled off in the gradually growing light. We lined up together on the strip, Chase on my left and slightly ahead. The mag check was perfect. I saw Chase's head, silhouetted, turn toward me and his ailerons flapped up and down. I rocked my stick right and left in answer, and immediately he started rolling and I crammed on throttle to stay with him. I watched him carefully, feeling the tug of power, playing the changing torque with the rudder pedals, but not seeing anything but that dark shape hurtling along in my left-forward vision. And suddenly everything became silky smooth and his wheels began tucking up under him, and I hooked my finger under the plastic guard and snapped up my toggle switch and heard the faint whine through the engine blast and felt the plane lift and come alive as the drag of the wheels was smoothed out. Some planes retracted their landing gear awkwardly. A P-40, for example, twisted its wheels sideways as it drew them back so they would fit into the wings. They looked as obscenely unnatural as a broken leg. But a P-39 drew its three wheels together and into its belly like a bird in flight. A lovely, yearning gesture that I cannot forget, as though the plane were wistful for the sky.

What a lot of crap, really. All a P-39 was actually wistful for was the ground.

Chase began the usual gentle turn to the right—toward me. Of course as I followed him, I drew toward him, so we made a tight two-plane unit as we finished that first turn. When he swung the other way to pick up course, I slipped under him and nuzzled against his left side. We climbed peacefully together, the air like glass, brightening as we rose with the still-distant sun. The ground below was almost black to us, a faceless mat of forest.

Chase noticed my position and waved me away a bit so I could see around me and not just stare at him to avoid colliding with him. I was relieved that my squadron used a broad patrol formation. We had heard that some wanted their ships tied together by a six-foot string, and that seemed crazy to us new men.

The mountains loomed nearer, silhouetted against the sunrise. I could look down now into steep-walled jungle valleys where morning mists lay as thick as cream. Just the place to find a last surviving pterodactyl winging off for a breakfast of saber-toothed tiger. What a place for an engine failure, I thought, and immediately my engine began to sound rough and uneasy. I knew that pilots often hallucinate and imagine things that are not so, but there was no mistaking this roughness. I peered at my engine gauges, which I could barely make out, and saw every needle on the green. Nervously, I settled back and tried to keep my eyes probing the sky above and behind Chase, the way I was supposed to.

Then I jumped to hear Chase's voice, very calm in my earphones: "Clear your gun."

I knew what to expect, for he had told me that it was a good idea to fire a few rounds of cannon when we were at altitude, so the breech mechanism wouldn't freeze up and quit. I snapped on the cannon selector switch and briefly pressed the trigger on the stick.

Whump-whump-whump. God, what a sensation.

And no sooner had I relished it than I saw a shocking thing straight ahead. Three unmistakable puffs of smoke, right on a line with my plane, some distance away. With a frantic reaction brought on by all those buried tensions, I jammed stick and rudder to one side, violently enough, almost, to produce a high-speed stall. The plane leapt up on one wing skittishly, like a street pigeon in a gust of wind. I pressed my microphone button and croaked "Ack-ack! Straight ahead!"

Rabbit's answer came back smoothly and laconically: "Your own shells, lamebrain."

Abashed, I fell back into formation. I had forgotten that 37-millimeter shells exploded if they didn't strike anything first. I kept a bit farther away from Chase so I wouldn't have to look him in the eye.

And at that point my plane laughed at me.

It was as simple as that: a clear, girly laugh right in my ears.

Goddamn this bitch, anyway, I thought. And just about then Rabbit waggled his wings to draw me closer, and then pointed ahead to where the low light showed a ragged pass in the mountains—a nearby height with an open expanse of lower ground stretching beyond. I watched Chase as he peered at it, then turned to me and made the thumb and finger ring that means all OK. His voice came into my earphones:

"Mary from Gopher Special, go ahead."

There was a pause, then a rasp of the carrier wave and a faint, staticky voice—Australian: "Gopher Special, this is Mary. Over to you."

Chase came back with that slightly strained pilot's voice that resulted from the contraption known as a throat mike—two little microphones designed to pick up a man's voice right straight from the Adam's apple. It invariably sounded garbled, so old-timers like Chase spoke very slowly and carefully:

"Mary from Gopher Special, Charlotte, Charlotte, Charlotte. Go ahead."

"Ah, this is Mary, Gopher Special. Understand Charlotte. Is that correct?"

"Roger, Mary. Charlotte."

"Thank you, Gopher Special. Out."

And by that time we had completed an easy 180 turn and were headed home. I found myself relaxing at last. Just drive on up there and turn around and drive back. Nothing to it.

"Gopher Special Two. Twelve o'clock high."

Jesus, that was *me*. With a great surge of adrenalin, I galvanized back into high tension. Let's see. Twelve o'clock means straight ahead and high means high . . . I peered angrily upward through my canopy, my plane quivering with every frightened pulse that beat through me. The sky was dark except for a bright white contrail that tapered to a tiny silver dot. I looked over at Chase. He was grinning at me. What did that mean? Should we climb all the hell and gone up there and attack? Was this far-off enemy going to drop on us like a falcon and blast us out of the air? What are we supposed to *do,* for God's sake?

Chase kept heading for home, perfectly calmly, still smiling. I grimly held my position, readying myself for immediate bloodstained action. The vapor trail passed serenely over us and then curved away toward the north. I watched it with excruciating care, expecting any moment to see it curl down to an attack. My plane suddenly began running very smoothly and I had to throttle back to keep from getting ahead of Chase.

In no time, it seemed, we were out of the mountains, dropping toward the sea. Chase's voice came on again:

"Mary from Gopher Special, go ahead."

"Go ahead, Gopher Special." The Australian voice was close and clear now.

"This is Gopher Special. We'll be with you in five. Out."

"Roger, Gopher. Out."

And then Chase swung a little to the left and I found myself looking at twelve lumbering C-47s, climbing slowly toward us, and above them two flights of P-39s—our own squadron. The rising sun was glinting on them all as they climbed and turned, the little fighters weaving to stay with the transports. A new voice intruded:

"Gopher Special from Gopher Red leader. We have you."

And Chase again: "Roger, Kev. See you later."

And so we swept past each other, we in a long downward slant, they rising and weaving, herding the transports northward. I looked at the 39s with awe. They all wore 110-gallon belly tanks—as we did—and somehow these protuberances destroyed some of the elegant curves, as advanced pregnancy does, and made the planes look formidable. I supposed that even I looked formidable. And for the first time that morning I smiled.

The silver dot at the head of the contrail that Rabbit and I saw that early morning turned out to be the only enemy plane sighted that day. Chase told me it was a Dinah, a twin-engined Japanese reconnaissance plane which could cruise at about 40,000 feet—far higher than anything we had.

"What was it doing?" I asked. "It wasn't light enough for photos."

Chase shrugged. "Could have been dropping a few bombs somewhere, I guess. I think they carry a couple. Anyway, I doubt if he even saw us, and we weren't about to tangle with him."

Later, when the escort missions returned, I was able to lord it over Lambert, one of my fellow replacements, who had been on the mission: "Yeah, a Dinah, coming back from a bomb run at about 40,000 feet. Too scared to get any lower."

Lambert was impressed.

Next morning I was scheduled again—this time for the escort mission. Beside my name on the posting was the number 74. I was Number Two man in Red Flight—flying wing on the squadron leader, who was my old friend Skunk-Ass that day.

"Your belly tank will last just about an hour and forty minutes," Skunk-Ass told me. "You can switch it a little before that. If you forget, it'll run out and then you can switch it—or glide right into a mountain."

We took off at sunrise, the plane feeling familiar to me as she gently swung away from the runway in that creamy smooth morning air. I had heard the distant, garbled call of the weather hop—Steve was Number Two on it this morning—and realized how neatly timed it was, for the transports were already circling above us when it came. As we started our engines, they straightened out on course. Within a few minutes our two flights were airborne, climbing after the C-47s. And the sun, coming up beyond the mountains, had distinct fanned rays like a Japanese flag. It seemed it must be an ominous sign that this was Japan's day, and I peered anxiously in all directions, almost willing myself to see distant spots against the paling northern sky, coming at us.

But there was nothing like that. We followed the same course as yesterday, above the same deep green valleys, past the same granite fangs. And 74 ran rough, palsied with strange vibrations deep within her entrails as soon as she saw the mountains below. Again, all the gauges were in the green.

It took far longer to reach the pass than it had on the weather hop. The C-47s labored upward—eighteen of them—two Vs of Vs—and we wove back and forth above them, keeping them always in view with one eye while the other searched the sky. At last there was the same saddle, and the transports below us seemed to scrape their bellies on it. Then their speed picked up as they slid down the other side into the valley where Chase and I had not gone.

It was a small valley with a diminutive range of hills bounding it on the north. Beyond them gleamed the sea, bright and seemingly calm as the sun glanced off it. A peninsula of steep-walled hills, all jungle-clad, jutted into it just off my nose, and I recognized it from the map in the alert tent: Salamaua. The knowledge sent the old adrenalin pumping afresh. This was the Japanese base that served as springboard for the attack on Wau. I waited fatalistically for the flash of giant antiaircraft guns, the blood-red burst of great shells blasting me from the sky. There was nothing. Just our two flights weaving and then widely circling as the transports broke into a long line, heading for a pale earthen strip slashed in the valley between the hills.

One by one, painfully slow in their approaches, the C-47s landed, paused to disgorge their troops, then began interspersing

each landing with a takeoff so no more than two planes were at
the high end of the strip at once. It was hair-raising to see them
almost pass each other, one sliding in to land uphill while another roared off the ground, downhill, then veered quickly to
the right to get out of the way. The burned-out wreck of a transport beyond the high end of the strip reminded everyone that if
you missed on your approach you couldn't go around and try
again. I thought about my engine failing, and whether I would
be able to get 74 onto that strip. And I knew that of course I
couldn't; I simply wasn't good enough to make a landing like
that on a short strip with a hot ship first time in.

Just then my engine quit cold.

The sudden absence of sound was shattering. Blind to all
thought, to all feeling, I found my left hand snapping down to
the fuel selector valve, twisting it from belly tank to left wing
tank. And with a pleasant roar old 74 started up again as if
nothing had happened. All that adrenalin, apparently, was doing
some good: I had reacted so quickly that I didn't even fall away
from formation.

I looked at my wrist watch. One hour and forty-two minutes
from takeoff. I had switched onto belly tank within about four
minutes from start-up. Skunk-Ass had been close enough. I
looked over at his cockpit appreciatively, and he was watching
me and made a twisting motion with his hand. I nodded, and he
waved. Skunk-Ass obviously knew a Dilbert when he saw
one.

Quite suddenly, the last transport, far below, was taking off,
and we followed it toward the pass, shepherding it as it caught
its place in the last V. And then, blessedly we were over the
pass ourselves, out of sight of all that dread, sun-drenched
enemy sea with its enemy islands dotting it and the awful,

enemy-sounding Salamaua Peninsula sticking out into it. Ahead was nothing but the diminishing mountains and the long, dreary rain-forested flatland and then the sea again on the horizon, pale blue at that distance. The country was far less beautiful in this direction, but at least it was ours.

For the first time a voice came into my earphones:

"Gopher leader from Tony, we have bandits, we have bandits." The Japs were hitting Wau. Right behind us.

And Skunk-Ass answered, "Sorry, Tony, no can do."

And that was that. We just flew on toward Moresby.

After we landed, I climbed into the hood of a jeep for a ride back to the alert tent. My gabardine flying suit was soggy with sweat and my legs were trembling. All eight of us were on the jeep, somehow, and all talking at once.

"Those bastards! Ten minutes more and we'd have hit them."

"Christ, why can't we get bigger belly tanks and stretch the range?"

"They ought to send the 38s in over us. They could stay on and clean 'em out."

I was astonished to hear my own voice taking part in the half-shouted imprecations as we jolted back to the alert tent. My common sense reminded me that the very last thing I really wanted was to somehow stumble into conflict with a Japanese plane, yet the reaction from the mission was a sense of such pleasure at still being alive that I was happy to go along with any outrageous idea.

That evening I found myself drinking whiskey beside Skunk-Ass and Airedale and being treated with cordiality. These, I realized, were all very nice young men, and if you stayed alive you would find them quite delightful. I had indeed stayed alive, and tomorrow I had a day off, and that left about thirty hours before I faced it again, and if I could keep that up for a year and a bit I would be sent back to the States. So far so good. I proceeded to get bombed with my new friends.

VI

The Gophers

Gopher Squadron was an old outfit—a two-digit squadron—
and had come out to the Philippines a year before Pearl
Harbor. It had been sent out from Selfridge Field, Michigan,
and there were still a handful of us—the CO, the operations officer, the engineering and armament officers, and a few of the
enlisted men—who remembered those peacetime days when you
wore army whites in the summer and called on your base commander and left your card on a mahogany table in the front hall.

It seemed strange that Jim, the CO, and Kev, the ops officer, in their sawed-off khaki pants and green Australian shirts and flopped-open flying boots, could ever have worn Sam Browne belts and snapped out salutes to MPs at the brick gates of an old army post. But they had, and they would sometimes talk about it, shyly, knowing that the rest of us would rib them mercilessly.

These few, unblessed with biological nicknames, had flown little P-26s back then, low-wing Boeings with wheels sticking down in streamlined pants. They could dance around the sky and they could line up in a long, wavering echelon for the cameraman at Pathé News and thus make everyone feel swell about American air power in 1937. Some of them very bravely went up against Zeros in the Philippines. That was the end of them.

Jim and Kev had been on P-39s by then, but Clark Field was hit so hard and so early that few fighter missions could get off the ground. I don't know what they did. They never talked about it except to shake their heads at the rest of us sometimes and tell us we should have been along when it was rough.

The majority of the old pilots—the animal kingdom—had come in from various scratch outfits when Gopher settled down in Sydney to rebuild and train for New Guinea. Many of these, almost a majority, came from the Royal Canadian Air Force. They told hilarious stories about flying Avro Anson trainers in Ontario where you had to wind up the wheels by hand—seventy-seven turns of the crank. By the time you got the gear up it was time to grind it down again. "We learned to fly all stooped over," Rabbit told me. "That's why we feel comfortable in a 39."

They also knew the world's dirtiest songs, picked up in Canada because some of the instructors were British, and the British are the fountainhead of all the dirty songs ever sung.

I listened with enjoyment to the talk at the bar, that night after my first full mission, and with delight to the harmonized strains of "Please Don't Burn Our Shit-house Down." With a sense almost of contentment, I recognized and accepted the small, honest cordialities extended toward us new men by the old hands. When they discussed, casually, the details of their work—moments during earlier missions when they had escaped death by some miraculous reaction and returned to the ground to hoot hilariously at their fortune—they left me stone-cold. I decided they were simply lying their heads off. Either that, or they were all insane. Yet when they talked about life back in the States, when they asked questions about what the girls were like, and who the hell did this Frank Sinatra think he was, and what was the latest top tune of the "Hit Parade," and what stars were winning Oscars, and what was it like to be short of gas, and, especially, what great meals had we eaten lately—that sort of question touched us all, and I answered as well as I could, with a growing understanding of their need to know. They seemed then merely familiar types, fun to drink with.

I was unassigned the next day, so slept late and had breakfast with Lambert. He was a quiet boy who had trained in another area and joined us at Charter Towers. This morning he was scheduled for the second flight, so he could eat a late breakfast (cold raw bacon, thick pancakes, hot, sweetened water, waxy imitation butter, coffee, and a limeade known as "battery acid") before going down to the line. He told me about his wife, which turned out to be the reason he was quiet, since he'd only been married a week when he went overseas. He said marriage was wonderful. "It really gives you a purpose," he said. "I never had any plans except to finish up all this lousy business, but now I'm thinking about ways to beat the Depression and maybe make a buck or two with what I'm learning."

"You mean like how to shoot a machine gun at a moving target?" I asked.

"Shit, you know what I mean. Look at what we're learning about flying—little narrow steel-matting strips to land on; all that pressure on getting off and on the ground fast. All that stuff would be great back in Arizona for flying dudes around."

It sounded good. "Hey, Lambert, hire me, Ok?"

He got up to go to the line. "It's a deal," he said.

Exactly twenty minutes later, he was dead. He had been taking off on that narrow little strip that he thought was teaching him so many neat things. He was flying Badger's wing, doing this newfangled two-ship takeoff that we were supposed to do, and he caught a piece of slipstream from Badger's plane and flipped onto his back, about ten feet off the ground. He didn't burn, so we had to bury him with a funeral next day. Steve and I then had the tent to ourselves. We used his bunk to dump our gear on and keep it out of the mud that formed when those big thunderstorms struck.

Steve was a New Yorker, a Greenwich commuter who had been spending his three years since graduation in running errands at his father's firm. "Do you *like* real estate?" I asked.

"No, but it's a job."

I understood, of course. The Depression was an utterly practical time when you thankfully grabbed whatever came your way and hoped that someday you would be able to change it for a more comfortable fit. Many young men chose the services for that difficult first employment—so many that the small army and navy of prewar days could get by with paying their enlisted men about a dollar a day. What the hell, you ate, didn't you? Those who could make it, whose eyesight was good and who reacted like cats, would try for flying. Again, quotas were kept so low that only the best of them got through. The results were the bright, dedicated young experts who made up the "old guys" in our squadron and in every other, army and navy. Only Pearl Harbor could have opened the gates to the flood of raffish, unmilitary, half-trained, ill-favored civilians that now flew.

Badger resented us. He was a midwesterner, devoted to flight as other people are to art. He flew with delighted absorption, as though approaching an orgasm with his sweetheart. He was gentle and loving with an airplane, and it responded to him by doing things you would hardly believe. When the squadron had left Sydney, I was told, the pilots were allowed to stage a modest display over Elizabeth Bay, which was where the leave-time flat was—and most of the girl friends. Badger, they say, got between the rooftops over one street and went blazing past, upside down, so his admirers were looking down on the belly of his plane. I can't vouch for that, but I watched him one day at New Guinea flying past the control tower—a little jerry-built affair no more than twenty-five feet tall—while Rabbit was taking movies of him. "How was that?" he asked Rabbit on ground frequency.

"That was OK, but how about trying an inverted pass?"

"Oh," said Badger. "OK."

By the time Rabbit had put the mike down and picked up the camera, Badger was on his way, below the level of the tower and upside down. His voice came over the speaker: "Better?"

Rabbit picked up the mike again. "You came so fast I didn't get a good shot. Try it again, but take it a little easy."

"OK."

And he made a turn way out and came back, this time throttled back as though he was going to land the plane. He rolled gently upside down and came mushing past the tower, his nose high, his tail almost dragging on the runway.

Rabbit hadn't realized he was going to do it inverted again. He kept the camera going, and then grabbed up the mike.

"That was swell, Badger. Please come in and land now."

"OK." And with a roar of power, Badger climbed the plane, still inverted, then did a quarter roll and crammed it around in a vertical bank inside the traffic pattern. His wheels and flaps popped open and he slipped down and around in a graveyard turn onto the strip. I don't think there was a moment when his airspeed got above eighty-five—which was just about the stall. But he got around just in time and laid it on the runway, one wheel still high, with a gentle rattle of the matting.

Badger was a hard man to take off with, as I soon learned. I was often assigned as his wingman, which meant we took off in element. And every time, just as my plane came free of the ground and started tucking up its wheels and trying to gain fly-ing speed, Badger would start a turn right into me. This meant that I had to turn with him, although I was slightly below him and hardly flying. My low wing would almost scrape the run-way as I banked with him. It was one of the hairiest situations I was ever in.

I did it once—wondering if this was what had happened to Lambert—and then the next time I flew with him I slipped under him as he turned. That was hairy, too, but at least it gave me a chance to build airspeed. With the needle in the fat I was able to zing around after him and slide back to the inside eche-lon position where I should be.

Badger didn't like it at all and said so after we landed. "What the fuck did you think you were doing on that takeoff?"

"I was saving my ass," I told him. "If you want to turn into your wingman go do it with someone else. I enjoy life."

"Shit, if you can't fly a fighter why aren't you in trans-ports?"

The idea was most appealing to me, except when I thought of those landings uphill at Wau. I would have preferred observation, maybe, in a navy float plane. All that good food. I shook off the happy dream and got back to being angry with Badger.

"Look, Badger, I never pretended to be able to fly a fighter. Obviously I can't. But as long as the army keeps on making this terrible mistake, I shall go on trying to stay alive. And that means you can take your fucking takeoffs and stuff them."

He grinned at me, and from that moment on he did his dirty little turn on takeoff, and I did my sleazy little duck under him.

The Wau escorts went on, day after day. The Nips, apparently were almost on the airstrip, so the transports were taking small arms fire as they landed, and the Australians would jump out and start shooting as soon as they hit the ground. And day after day, just after we had reached the point of no return on our way home, Tony would call us to say the bandits were coming in, and we would say, "Sorry," and drive on home.

VII

Falling in Love

I flew Number 74 a great deal. I began to understand her. I knew that she hated to take off with Badger, but would do it, wrenching herself off the ground and squeezing under him as he turned into her and then panting after him, all with the blind desperation that I used to feel when I forced myself to climb to the thirty-foot platform on the raft at the lake and then leap off it simply because my peers were doing it. The old cold-shower syndrome. I appreciated what 74 was going through and I would

74

talk to her during that takeoff, joshing her along and telling her it wasn't really so bad. Pretty soon I got to calling her Nanette.

I have no idea why the name came to me. It sounded sort of whorey, and yet insouciant, that mixture of intensive self-service and innocent enjoyment that she had been revealing to me with increasing candor as we flew together. For never did I mount her cockpit without her making some demand of me, a small thing, usually—like slipping to one knee on the wet dew as I climbed her wing—but just enough to remind me that she was emotionally independent of me, that she was doing me a favor by submitting to me, and had I tucked the money under the pillow?

And then, as the flight proceeded, she would indicate in a hundred ways that as long as it was going the way she wanted it to go—nice and straightforward, without any disgusting perversions like shooting off her guns at enemy planes—she would not only give me a good ride, but would thoroughly enjoy it herself. She would hum lightheartedly as she danced through her maneuvers. Oh, yes, perhaps she would be grumpy for half an hour if she had the wing position on Badger—she would clear her throat testily as we crossed the mountains. But always, on the way home, safely out of range of the ubiquitous bandits of Wau, she would lose her nervousness and purr gently.

When, as was often the case, the squadron leader for the day would lead us through the writhing corridors and bulging domes of afternoon cumulus in a joyful, hilarious rat race, Nanette would fling herself into it with sweet abandon. She and I would wheel around a sunlit castle of cloud, dipping our wings into its creamy walls, soaring up to rub the pulsing top away from its highest watchtower, then howling down through its passages, following the plane ahead, followed by the next in the flight, slow-rolling as we dove, until we saw the dark dungeon below—which proved to be our own earth after all. Nanette would play delightedly, climbing eagerly, dropping a wing to pirouette, plunging and rolling in a crescendo of excitement.

And when it was over, and we were headed homeward in tight echelon, going flat out and kicking up dust with our props, she would slip into another mood, seeming to concentrate on a proper ending to the ball. We would smash over the strip, then flick up and to the left so suddenly that we tweaked a wispy contrail from the outside wing tip. A thousand feet high, we would sink and turn all at once, fading away toward the ground, finally reaching for it with the whistling landing gear. And then there would be the tiny final touch, the rattle of the matting, the quick taxiing to the revetment, the wind-down of the propeller. And I would leave her with a pat on her cowl—she as flushed and breathless as I.

VIII

Living Machines

I was brought up with a Buick named Bella. She was almost exactly the same age as I was, but matured faster, as cars do, so that I never learned to drive her except to rumble jerkily around the yard once in a while. She grew to be a great lady, beautiful and still rakish in her old age, dignified yet forgiving, above all devoted to our family. She was dark green, a touring car with her black top usually down because we only drove her in the summers. She had black leatherette seats that got hot when she was parked in the sun and picked up pine needles when we left her in the shade. One of my brothers painted a thin pale blue line around her tonneau, coming to within an inch of the tops of her doors, and on each door the line curled into a little design that framed our initials—my sister's, my two brothers', and my own.

No one had to put Mother's and Dad's initials on Bella because she was unquestionably theirs anyway. It was my mother who brushed the pine needles off the seats and loaded her with belongings for the trip from Boston up to New Hampshire in June and back to Boston in September. It was my father who best understood her six thundering great cylinders and who would grit his teeth in shared effort as he worked her up to forty-five miles an hour in order to take a hill on high—celebrating success by kicking the muffler cutout so that she blatted in triumph as she cleared the crest.

Bella got old and ill finally, and my father wrestled with his emotions and decided to sell her to Dyer Brown, the garageman who knew her as well as we did. We didn't want it to happen, but we couldn't see a way out.

But Bella could. When Dyer drove up to our place to get her, she died. She was driving up from the barn, and abruptly she stopped—a massive fracture of an integral part.

Dyer Brown understood completely. He surveyed the relic in the driveway, looked at my father oddly and said, "Bruk her Goddamn heart."

Heart, maybe. But not her soul. A couple of years later one of my older brothers came home from learning how to fly in the marines—this was Depression, and no kid just out of Yale with a BS in engineering could hope to get a job, so a lot went into the services to get in on the glamor and good pay of aviation— and he went down to the graveyard behind the barn and kicked thoughtfully at Bella's gently rotting corpse and said, "Come on, we're going to take her engine out."

Having learned early to do what my brothers told me, I helped him rig a log tripod, and we hooked up a sixteen-to-one block and tackle and yanked the old monster out and on to Katy Ford's flatbed. And then we raised it again in the barn and got it on some horses, and my brother spent the rest of the summer grinding the valves and putting in new rings. And my father built a new little woodshed up by the house and set a bed for Bella's engine beside it—a frame of eight-by-eight timbers on concrete foundation posts. And he bought a saw frame and arbor for sawing firewood.

Finally, we all managed to get Bella's engine, clean and oily, onto the bed and loop a heavy belt from the clutch to the arbor. And one September morning when my mother and sister came out to watch, my brother cranked away at Bella and my father played the choke and I stood by with more gas to feed into the carburetor. And suddenly with a great bellow of unmuffled triumph, she fired up. We released the clutch, and the bright new saw sang as it spun, and when we tried a stick of gray birch, the saw spoke briefly above Bella's thunder.

We all looked at each other and knew we wouldn't have to use the two-man crosscut anymore. We shut down Bella and sniffed the exquisite smell of Bella's pollution in the clear country air. We felt that this was what human beings were all about.

I mentioned Katy Ford. She was a handsome little thing who could be converted from roadster to pickup truck and back again as quickly as you could handle the wrench. So we used her to take the garbage can down to the pit in the woods east of the house, or to pick up a load of gravel from the bank on the hill or to haul trimmed birch trunks over to the saw. And in the evenings, my brother would clean her up and replace the flatbed with the little boot and go bouncing down the driveway to pick up his date. Katy did whatever was asked of her in the best of humor. She was warm and affectionate and when you cranked her she tended to nudge her hot little radiator into your stomach. You'd have to push her back and tell her to cut it out, damn it. And she'd start up with a chuckle and sit there panting while you climbed up onto the high seat. "What fun and excitement have you got in store for me now?" she would ask. Frivolous, Katy was, but a real sweetheart.

My aunt's Ford was Elijah, and my father would draw in his breath and shake his head sorrowfully whenever he saw poor old Elijah stop at the door with my aunt in control. She wasn't very mechanical and she developed a technique for stopping Elijah that was not very good for him. On a Model T there were three foot pedals. The left one, pushed halfway down, threw out the clutch. Pushed all the way down it dropped the car into low gear. The center pedal was reverse. The right was the brake. Now all that was sort of complicated for my aunt, so if she needed to stop suddenly—and she was the kind of driver who *always* needed to stop suddenly—she simply stamped down at random. There would be this shriek of tortured gears and poor Elijah would haul up like a hound meeting a skunk. Of course his engine would stall and he would sit there ticking nervously while the other driver, or the owner of the tree, or the pedestrian with the shopping bag, or the cop with the raised hand would say some fairly rotten things to my aunt.

Henry Ford must have had a lot of frailties back when he was designing Katy and Elijah. Their marvelous imperfections indicated clearly that they had inherited strains of nervous energy, of bad temper, of haughty manners, of warmth and affection, of unseen strength and sudden, senseless fear. Life was the better for such machines.

Larry Bell, too, must have been pleasantly imperfect. He designed a plane that reflected a most shaky heritage—sloppy, lazy, self-indulgent, all those good, familiar faults. And also beautiful. His Airacobras all bore this slanderous family resemblance, and those of us who flew them all shared, I think, a sort of comfort at being so closely associated with such warmly familiar creatures in so wildly unfamiliar an environment.

I, who was fully and unceasingly terrified by my unbelievably dangerous prospects on that lovely, deadly tropical island, found great comfort in Nanette. This one member of the Bell family had somehow acquired all the scourings of the gene pool. All the family tendencies were in her exaggerated. Where other Airacobras were handsome and demanding, she was breathtakingly radiant and absolutely vicious. Where others were merely inadequate at their job, she was a sloven. Where others could always put on a good show if absolutely necessary, she could dazzle. Where others quailed noticeably at flying combat missions in New Guinea, she shook with uncontrolled panic. Moreover, bless her rotten heart, she recognized in me a fellow poltroon and clung to me determinedly.

IX

Scrambling

On a bright morning about a month after joining the squadron, we were all called to the alert tent and told to stand by for a scramble. The primitive radar was apparently pulsing with strange blips—most of these usually turned out to be thunderstorms—and word from the coast watchers indicated that the Japanese had gathered some extra bomber strength at Lae, on the north coast, and that they might be headed this way.

Nanette ordinarily enjoyed scrambles. The idea was to dash

out to your plane, usually clinging to the fender of a jeep, zipping your raggedy old flying suit up over your hacked-off khaki shorts and slipping into your greasy leather shoulder holster with its huge, useless Colt automatic gradually rusting away in it. And then you would leap onto the wing of your plane and your crew chief would lasso you with your Mae West and shove you into your seat. By the time he had jumped down you had the energizer winding up, and the minute the engine came to life you would start rolling toward the end of the strip, meanwhile clipping on your parachute as fast as you could. And as the planes came together in pairs, they would waggle ailerons at each other, and off they'd go, never pausing to check the mags or the prop pitch—two, four, six, eight, and so on into the air, circling and climbing and crawling together into position.

Nanette always behaved beautifully at these times, for there was something silly about them that tickled her. Here were all these guys who had been playing bridge or solitaire on the folding cots only a matter of seconds before, now struggling to snap the last snaps and buckle the last buckles and get their testicles comfortable and still fly these dicey little planes into a formation that would perhaps look formidable to an approaching enemy. Nanette would purr with pleasure and slide me neatly into my slot, lifting strongly, obviously smiling. After all, there was never a reason for these scrambles—just a thunderhead. It was like having boat drill on the *Queen Mary* along with that Vassar girl you danced with last night.

But this time, Nanette was very nervous. She flamed up from her exhaust stacks when I started her, and she coughed nastily when I hit the throttle for takeoff. I swore at her and jammed her into the air, and she wandered straight into someone's prop wash and dipped a wing rather dangerously. And then she seemed to resent climbing into formation. She seemed simply angry at having been waked up, but I knew her well enough to realize that she was showing her own symptoms of panic.

This, of course, was enough to put me into a tizzy, and I flew sort of jerkily beside Rabbit so that he glanced over at me with a quizzical look above his oxygen mask.

The radio was crackling with voices. Our own sector came through very clearly: the Australian voice, Mary, calling Teeny and Madam and, by God, Gopher. "Vector nine five, Gopher, at angels one two." That meant fly roughly eastward at 12,000 feet. We were still under ten and increased the climb. Nanette complained.

Then there were many other very faint voices fading in and out. There were snatches of messages; disjointed phrases: ". . . from Peter, vector one three five . . . One eight . . . about seventy-five . . ." and then a lot of crackling. Then another voice: ". . . three o'clock, Skeeter leader . . . NO, NO, don't drop your tanks, don't drop . . ." More static. I began to sweat in the chill of the cockpit as we reached 12,000 feet. And suddenly, quite clearly, a very excited voice: "I got the bastard!"

I knew that Peter was the code name for Milne Bay, a base at the eastern tip of the island. I also knew that the 39s would have range enough to get there and back and even rat-race around for a bit, though it might be a stretch to do it all without the belly tanks. I found myself breathing very hard and saying "Jesus—Jesus—Jesus—" over and over into my oxygen mask. Nanette was simply hanging into formation with a sort of desperation. We flew inexorably toward the action, and the voices came in clearer and clearer.

"Skeeter leader from Peter, bandits should be nine o'clock to you. Nine o'clock."

"Roger, Peter. Thank you."

"Peter from Madam, we will be in your area shortly, angels one eight. Over."

"Madam leader from Peter, roger, understand angels one eight. Bandits will be below you."

Madam was our P-38 squadron. Skeeter was a P-40 outfit from Milne Bay. The 38s had the speed to get to the scene. I fervently hoped that we couldn't. So did Nanette.

We zinged along at 12,000 feet, the jungle unrolling prettily under us, the ocean on our right, the mountains on our left. I felt so full of adrenalin that if I moved it would slosh.

And then glorious words: "Peter to all flights, the bandits have left us. We are all clear. We are all clear."

Oh, joy. Oh, gratitude.

But my rapture was interrupted by Rabbit's voice. He was squadron leader that day. "Gopher from Gopher leader, keep your eyes peeled for intercept." And he began a gentle turn toward the mountains, climbing slightly.

What the hell was wrong with him, I wondered. Couldn't he leave well enough alone? Why did he have to go scrounging around for trouble? I made my turn with Rabbit and glared at the sky with hot eyes. If the Nips were headed back to Lae they would almost certainly pass in front of us and give us a good chance at an intercept. I squinted at various sections of sky, trying to make out the distant specks.

And with dreadful clarity—*there they were!* Unmistakably, eight tiny shapes flicked out of the edge of a cloud and began a gentle turn—*in our direction.*

I reacted with blistering speed, cramming down my mike button, which was on the throttle handle, and pressing the twin disks of the throat mike against my Adam's apple: "Gopher leader, bogies at''—let's see, if I'm in the middle of the clock where the hell are those planes? Oh, yes—I've got it—"ten o'clock level.''

My voice was almost lost in a babble of others, all calling in frantically. And then there was a pause in the carrier-wave hums, and another voice came in strongly:

"Gopher leader from Madam. Believe you have sighted us. Believe we have you at ten o'clock. Can you identify?'' And with that, the distant shapes banked vertically in formation and revealed the twin booms of P-38s.

"Thank you, Madam,'' said Rabbit, calmly. "We see you.'' And then, at long last, "Let's head for the barn, boys.''

I had been struggling to keep Nanette in some sort of decent formation where I could support Rabbit if we hit the Nips, but that recalcitrant whore fought me, holding back, shying away from position, sagging off, as though to dive for the deck, blindly. Now, as we turned again toward our strip, she smoothed out and perched immovably on Rabbit's wing, as though glued into position.

We began a long, shallow dive, howling with speed, and I saw Rabbit undo his oxygen mask and rub the sweat from around his mouth and nose. Then he fingered a cigarette out of his breast pocket and stuck it between his lips. Then he searched for a match. Uselessly. Finally he looked over at me, pointed to his unlit cigarette, made the gesture of striking a match and held out his gloved hand beside his window. I had a book of matches and I produced them and held them up. He nodded eagerly and beckoned me to come closer. Nanette slid up beside him until her wing tip was almost next to his cockpit—about a yard out. Rabbit watched with a pleased smile, then shook his head and gestured a shrug. I saw him grip his throat mike.

"Thanks anyway,'' he said.

A few minutes later we were on the ground, sweating, trembling, all talking at once, and I tossed Rabbit my matches and told him to keep them.

We had a briefing that evening beside the bar in the farmhouse. Jim, the CO, held a glass of the green-label Pennsylvania rye that was issued to us and gestured with it as he talked. "Our friends are pretty sure to visit again tomorrow," he said. "They don't get all that strength together just for one shot at Milne Bay. Elkhart says they've got about sixty bombers all lined up at Lae, according to the coast watcher, and so it looks as if we'll be scrambled again. Anyway, the milk run to Wau has been canceled so we stand by. You got anything, Kev?"

The ops officer looked up from where he was sitting. "The flights are just being posted," he said. "Mostly, it will be the same setup as today except for Park. I just found out that 74's losing oil, so you'll get another ship. Nailor, you'll fly in yellow flight. . . ." And so on. As soon as he was finished I moved over to the bulletin board and found my name with "75" beside it. I knew perfectly well what caused Nanette's oil leak. Cowardice.

Number 75 had been assigned to me before. A P-400, that export model which the RAF had wisely turned down. It sat in the next revetment to Nanette, and in the morning, after putting my chute and Mae West in place, I walked over to see Nanette's crew chief. He had an unpronounceable Polish name, so I called him John. He had Nanette's engine cowling unbuttoned and the big Allison was exposed. It was still too dark to see well. He was standing on a ladder, peering into her guts with a flashlight.

"Find anything?" I asked.

He looked around. "Hi, Lieutenant," he said. "Haven't found anything yet, but she wouldn't hold pressure when I ran her up last night."

"I know what's wrong with her," I said. "She's scared of hitting the Nips."

John nodded matter-of-factly. "That's it, all right. She's kind of a strange one," he said.

"Yeah," I said. "See you, John."

"Good luck, Lieutenant."

I walked back to the alert shack. It was sort of nice to know that John knew about Nanette and me.

The sun came up, and we unzipped our flying suits and sat or lay on the cots, trying not to listen for the jangle of the field telephone at Kev's desk. Someone wound up the Victrola and put on "San Antonio Rose." Rabbit was near me, sharpening his sheath knife. Steve lay on a cot, reading the overseas edition of *Time*. I dealt a hand of solitaire with some greasy cards. I could tell the ace of clubs because a corner was missing.

A truck rolled up to the shack and someone called out, "Smoko!" That was our squadron word for the morning coffee break. The Australians called it that. Some squadrons called it "Kai Kai," which was Pidgin English for food. We rolled off the cots and walked out into the heat, unhooking our canteen cups. A sergeant filled them from a great black pot in the back of the truck. I put in some sweetened condensed milk, picked out an ant, stirred, and drank a couple of swallows.

The phone rang.

For a moment there was absolute silence, as though we were all abruptly in some sort of time lag. No motion, no sound except "San Antonio Rose." Then the ops officer's voice through the tent flap: "Gopher Squadron. . . . Twenty-*three?* Right."

He appeared at the tent flap, and we all stared at him.

"Scramble all flights," he said. "Angels twenty-three over the area."

Pandemonium. A rush for the tent where some guys had left

their shoulder holsters. Canteen cups clattering into the bed of the truck as we dumped our coffee and tossed them toward the mess sergeant. Jeep engines racing. "San Antonio Rose" plaintively running down on the Victrola.

I flung myself onto the hood of a moving jeep that Rabbit was driving and we roared off for Red Flight's revetments, 200 yards away. Guys dropped off as they passed their planes and started running toward them, holsters flapping. Crew chiefs were all on the wings, hauling the pilots up, slapping the Mae Wests over their heads. I leapt off for 75, and the crew chief yanked me aboard and lassoed me the same way. Strap under crotch, around, and click. Helmet and goggles hanging on the control stick as I struggled into the cockpit and twisted my shoulders into the parachute straps. Snap; wrench; heave; click. Helmet on, goggles up, radio leads into the battery outlet: click, click. Oxygen mask hanging loose from the helmet: hose connection into the oxygen outlet: click. Switches on with a swipe of the hand. Heel on the energizer. Whine building up. Left hand tweaking throttle and mixture control while right is shoving down primer. Jesus Christ, there's Rabbit's plane already taxiing out in a swirl of dust. Toe on engager. Prop wheeling, coughing. Pat on knee from crew chief before he slams door and jumps clear with a wave. Plane rolling out behind Rabbit. Bouncing to end of runway at fifty miles an hour. Rabbit rolling into position. Planes converging now from every revetment. Piss-Ant beside me. Crossing himself in the cockpit. Crossing himself, for God's sake. Rabbit starting to move. Full throttle. Hope this crate doesn't quit on takeoff. Off the ground; wheels up; switch to belly tank; gentle turn; cool air from a vent somewhere; time at last to buckle up last straps, inch ass around to get it comfortable.

We climbed steeply, circling lazily around Port Moresby. The air was still and clear, but the earphones were jumping with talk.

"Binky from Mary, vector three six oh at angels two three. What are your angels now, Binky? Over."

A garbled answer.

"Roger, Binky. Vector two seven oh until you have angels two three. Over."

"Wilco."

"Madam from Mary, are you at one eight queen? Over."

"Roger, Mary. One eight queen at angels two oh."

"Roger, Madam. Keep a sharp lookout. Gopher from Mary, give me your position, please. Over."

Jim's voice. "Mary from Gopher, we are at one seven queen, angels one nine, vectoring two seven oh to one eight oh."

I had been too intent to realize that the CO was leading the squadron. My Red Flight was usually lead flight, but the scramble had called for all flights, so Jim and Kev and a couple of other off-duty men must have put together a special flight—usually called a "Gray" flight. I realized how badly we were strung out—just a parade of flights, spiraling steeply upward from left to right.

My plane was feeling mushy, inching above her normal ceiling. Twenty-one thousand feet . . . twenty-one five . . . twenty-one eight . . . twenty-two . . .

Suddenly, very loud in the earphones: "Gopher leader from Gopher Yellow Three, three o'clock level."

I snapped my head to the right and saw a strange speckling in the distance, as though someone had flicked a wet paintbrush against a landscape of building clouds. It took a moment before I could accept that these were planes—what seemed like masses of them—banked in a gentle turn over the gentle coastline, four miles below. Rabbit's plane swung toward them, and I followed carefully. And then when I looked again, the blobs had become twin-engine bombers with high tails, quite dark against the clouds, moving fast. And from the ground far below them, three distinct columns of brown, billowing smoke rose in the still air.

The radio hammered at my ears with excited voices, but I turned down the volume and watched with amazement as Rabbit's belly tank suddenly flipped from his plane and tumbled earthward. Quickly, I switched my selector and yanked my tank release, and the plane suddenly took on life and was able to climb again and dance in the sky instead of hanging on her propeller, straining for altitude.

From above the bombers a streak of smoke was suddenly penciled downward, then stopped—just a single dark line of smoke. And ahead of it, causing it, I saw a P-38 rocketing almost through the enemy formation. I knew then that the smoke must be from its guns.

And instantly the same thing streamed from Rabbit's plane: a rippling sheet of brown smoke. I swiped on my gun switches, tweaked the rheostat for the gunsight and, as the circle of light appeared on my windscreen, fired, I didn't fire *at* anything particular, although the bombers were more or less in my sight. I just frantically squeezed the trigger.

The cockpit filled with choking smoke as the 20-millimeter cannon blatted away between my legs. Then I realized that Rabbit was gone from beside me and I stopped shooting and clawed up and to the left after him. It seemed to me that he had broken off too soon. How could anyone expect to hit anything with a little burst at long range?

I caught Rabbit in a tight turn, and we went in again on the bombers, leveling into a shallow dive. Another P-38 slammed

down through them, trailing gun-smoke, and this time one of
the bombers was falling behind the rest. There was a faint line
of smoke from one engine.

Rabbit and I went in on this fellow, quite nicely together. I
began to feel pretty good about it all, to my surprise. I enjoyed
the sense of speed and lightness that resulted from the lack of a
belly tank, and it seemed sort of good fun to chase around the
sky on a nice bright day, shooting machine guns at a big black
target.

Rabbit fired at the straggler, and I joined in. Out of the corner
of my eye I saw Rabbit's plane flick away as he broke off. This
time, I held on a little longer, fascinated by the red curving
flight of my own tracers, intent on laying them into the target. It
was now quite near: high-tailed, angular, the sun glinting on the
flight-deck canopy. It wasn't black at all. It was dark green with
a dark red circle on the side of the fuselage. And I thought now
that I saw a couple of flashes along its length . . . .

Hastily, I snapped the plane away, turning and climbing in a
nicely coordinated flying school chandelle. This was really *fun!*
No wonder these guys all talked about combat with such relish.
Now to tighten up and pick up Rabbit again, and have another
go at it.

There was a sudden strange sound, a tinny rattling like a burst
of hail on a metal roof. Puzzled, I scanned my instrument panel
and saw every engine gauge in the green. I looked out at my
wings and then looked again. Something odd there. The smooth
contour on my right wing was broken by a sort of cratering effect. What the devil could that be?

It was suddenly quite clear what it could be. Bullet holes,
that's what. Those low-life bastards in that bomber had been
shooting a machine gun at me, for Christ's sake! What a sav-

age, dangerous thing for them to do! It would serve them right if I hit them the way they hit me!

I jammed the plane around angrily and started back at the bombers, all alone. And then an uncomfortable feeling asserted itself and my anger drained off. I looked again at the wings, uneasily. There were a lot of holes. There were some in the left wing as well as the right.

Uncertainly, I turned away and circled. The engine gauges still showed normal, and the plane sounded fine. But golly, those holes . . .

It began to seem powerfully urgent that I get back on the ground if I could. It also became very clear that I should not be alone like this, although all the neck-craning I could manage didn't reveal any other enemy planes. Still a little hesitantly, I eased off throttle and let the plane spiral down, lazily, toward the three tall columns of smoke that marked Moresby.

Abruptly another plane appeared, flying toward me. In some panic, I swung toward it, and instantly it went into a steep bank, turning to show me the white star on the wing. I waggled my wings (rather gently, for fear they would fall off) and we slid into formation with each other, the other man trying to fly wing on me, while I was trying to fly wing on him. But I felt that poor old Number 75 was in no shape to argue with anyone, so I ended up leading this strange little element of two frightened pilots.

My friend—it was a P-40 with a red nose which meant it was from Binky Squadron—stuck with me as we dropped toward the base. Then with a wave he left me for his strip. Some new pilot—I never found out who.

I slid carefully into our traffic pattern and came in for a landing. On the approach, I saw to my horror that another plane was landing in the other direction, coming right at me. Too late to do anything. I landed, very nicely for once, and taxied along on the right-hand side of the strip, and he whisked past me like a car on the Merritt Parkway.

My plane slowed her landing run, and I turned off for the revetment. Out of the corner of my eye I was aware of two trucks turning beside me, and I turned my head to look. Both, of course, were olive drab; one a flatbed which the squadron used as a fire engine, the other a panel van with a red cross on the side. They fell in just behind me as I taxied to the revetment. The crew chief brought me into position the way they do—like a symphony conductor—and signaled "cut" with a swipe of his flat palm across his throat. My own crew chief, John, stood beside him. I chopped off the mixture control and switched off. Instantly my door was open and there was John leaning in.

"For Christ's sake, don't smoke," he said. "You OK, Lieutenant?"

"Sure," I said.

"Then come on out and look at your airplane."

"I got some holes in it, huh?"

"I think it's broken, Lieutenant."

He helped me off the wing, for my knees were strangely weak. There was a strong smell of high octane gasoline. There was a steady dripping sound. Gasoline was pouring from the left wing, splattering on the ground. The wing was pocked with bullet holes.

The other crew chief handed me a small steel-coated object. "That's a Jap seven-point-seven bullet, sir," he said. "I just dug it out of the propeller blade."

I walked around the plane. There was a big bullet hole in the nose section—right through the number.

"Jap twenty-millimeter did that," said John. "There's another in the engine compartment. Guess they didn't explode."

"Guess not," I said.

"You made a nice landing, Lieutenant," said the other crew chief. "Considering."

I looked at him, and he nodded his head toward the nose wheel. The tire was flat.

"Right main, too," he said.

I glanced at the right main wheel and saw that the rubber had almost been torn off it.

The right wing was also riddled.

There were two bullet holes, one on each side of the cockpit, entering the wing fairing from the rear. "Both of them about six inches from your ass," as John pointed out.

I walked away silently, a bit unsteadily. John followed. A jeep was coming out from the alert tent, driven by the intelligence officer, Elkhart. I went to meet it, passing my own revetment, where Nanette brooded behind her earthworks, the sun glinting on her, highlighting those beautiful lines.

"She's OK now," said John behind me. "There was nothing much wrong with her."

"I know," I said.

I looked at her for a moment, and she looked at me. Just looked. Elkhart swung up in his jeep, and I climbed wearily in beside him.

X

Prospects

They counted 144 bullet holes in Number 75, and decided to junk her. I learned about it that night while I was drinking in the farmhouse. Jim came over and told me, and then he said, "You know how the Nips are scoring you, don't you? A probable. Maybe even a victory."

My plane was one of four which the squadron lost in the battle. Balz, a new pilot in Blue Flight, had been shot up by a Zero and bailed out over the harbor, neatly heading his smoking plane out to sea and then guiding his chute to a soft beach. He was drinking with me now. Airedale and Python were both missing. And my plane was junk. For this price we claimed two Betty bombers down and hits on a third. The straggler that got me had been downed, finally, by the 38s of Madam Squadron. They didn't have time to claim me.

I found it easy, that evening, to join in the squadron talk, shrill and neurotic though it was. For once, I had something to say ("It sounded just like hail on a tin roof!") and swooping gestures to make. The others listened with neither respect nor contempt, but with interest. I was describing things that they might meet up with tomorrow or the next day.

Poor old Number 75 was cannibalized for other planes, including Nanette. I hadn't liked 75 particularly because P-400s were weird to fly. But she had absorbed a lot of hard metal that had been headed right for my soft little body, and in spite of it all she had gotten me safely back on the ground. I was grateful to her and tried to make this clear to Termite when he came back from leave. She had been his plane.

Termite would have been flying 75 that day if he hadn't been 3,000 miles away, down in Sydney. He arrived home to the squadron a week after the combat, lugging a parachute bag full of great brown bottles of Australian beer and long salamis and bolognas and thick wedges of cheese, all wrapped in greasy paper. His friends gathered in his tent to say hello, and I went too because after all Termite was in Red Flight, and anyway I had something to break to him.

Some guys, coming back from leave, were more stingy with their loot than others, though no one was allowed to squirrel away beer and food just for himself. Termite was always generous, and he gestured for my canteen cup and slobbered it full of frothing dark beer, still cold from lying in the luggage bay of a

C-47 at 10,000 feet, and knifed over a chunk of salami and cheese. People were happily slurping and gnawing and saying, "Hey, Termite, didja get any?" That was an all-purpose squadron expression, used in reference to enemy planes, food, good things in general. In Termite's case, of course, it referred to poontang.

"Hey, Termite," I said. "I got something to tell you."

He looked at me curiously, a piece of cracker sticking out from his mustache.

"I flew your plane during our soiree last week," I began, using our squadron slang for combat.

"Didja get any?" Termite asked. No one laughed, because attention was on me.

"I—uh—got clobbered."

Attention swung to Termite. "You OK?" he asked. And then, "You mean my plane?"

I nodded.

"Oh, gee," he said very softly—in mourning. "How bad?"

"Bad. I'm afraid they junked her."

"Oh, *gee.*" He was silent for a while, though talk began quietly picking up around the two of us. Absently he drank a swallow of beer, and I, watching him, did too.

"She wasn't a bad little ship," he said, "even though she was a 400."

"I liked her," I said. "She got me home with all that stuff in her." I told him more about it.

"Yeah," he said. "She really saved your ass, didn't she?" He finished his beer and poured himself some more. Then he reached the bottle over and filled my cup.

"Maybe they'll give me one of the new N models," he said. Then suddenly, looking up, "You dumb bastard, Park. Getting clobbered by a Goddamn bomber.'' We both cut ourselves another chunk of salami.

Three days later we were all in the alert shack, playing cards and sharpening sheath knives, and the Victrola was playing ''San Antonio Rose,'' and a jeep pulled up outside and we heard a voice thanking someone and an Australian voice answering, ''That's arrright, mite.'' And in walked Airedale.

He was wearing a new set of Australian jungle greens, and he carried his canteen and pistol and his empty parachute pack, carefully rolled up and wound with long strands of the shrouds. He looked ten years younger—his cheeks filled out like a boy's.

It turned out that during the soiree he had chased a straggler right up to the mountains and then got hit from behind by a Zero. ''The engine quit, and I flipped off the door and rolled out,'' he said excitedly, glad to see us again and to tell about his adventure. We knew he must have been telling it in his head for ten days. ''I saw the Nip go after my ship. He was an Oscar, bright pink with green splotches. He blew my ship up. I guess he never saw me hit the silk.''

Elkhart was taking notes. Airedale waited until he had caught up. He was thoroughly enjoying himself. ''I came down in the trees. I crossed my legs and put my arms around my face the way they tell you and I slipped right through, almost to the ground before the chute hung up. And there were two Boongs already there. They cut me down.''

He told about how he knew the natives were OK because they were wearing Australian shorts. They were ''mission boys'' and they took Airedale to their village.

He tried out the bits of Pidgin English we had been taught— ''Me number one man belong lik lik balus; balus belong mefelleh e bugger up finish'' (which meant you flew a fighter which had pranged)—but mostly they just smiled at him and stared at him and fed him. "Christ," he said, "they fed me pork and fruit and breadfruit and more pork. Why can't *we* get chow like that?"

They moved him back toward Moresby, carrying him in a litter from village to village, though he could walk just as well as anyone. He said whenever he arrived at a new village, everyone there would be out waiting for him, though he never saw any way that they could have known he was coming: no runners, no drums. Each afternoon he would be transferred to the next village and fed on pork and breadfruit and bananas and pawpaws and put in the best house for the night.

"Didja get any?" someone asked. Airedale ignored him.

Two nights ago an Aussie patrol showed up in the village he had reached, and Airedale said that then the fun was over because the diggers made him hike along with them and fed him their rations. "Eighteen miles a day and the same shit we eat here," he said. "I said, 'Hey, you guys, I'm a downed pilot. Let's take it easy.' And they said I was fuckin' lucky they weren't fuckin' commandos, knocking off twenty-five fuckin' miles a fuckin' day."

When they got Airedale to their base, the Australian medics checked him over and he found he had gained twelve pounds.

Elkhart looked up from his notebook. "You'll get checked again tomorrow," he said. "And then the procedure is to send you down on leave."

Airedale looked stunned with happiness. "I get a ten-day rest cure and then Sydney on top of that, all for getting jumped by an Oscar and losing a hundred thousand bucks worth of airplane. You can't beat the Air Corps." He took a pull from the bottle of squadron rye someone had produced. "Where's Python?" he asked. "How long did it take him to get back?"

"He's not back," Jim said.

"But he bailed out practically over Fourteen-Mile Strip," Airedale said.

"Did you see him?"

"Sure. He was Tail-ass Charlie in White Flight, just ahead of us in Yellow Flight. I had swung the element wide and we were pretty close behind him when he just rolled over and went out. I saw the chute pop. Didn't you see it, Riznik? You were on my wing."

"I saw lots of stuff that day, but not that." Riznik was in my group of replacements. Good pilot.

"He never called in or anything," Jim said. "Radio must have been out."

"Did you see him land?" Kev asked Airedale.

"No, but he couldn't have been more than a mile or two off the end of Fourteen-Mile."

"What got him, could you tell?"

Airedale shook his head. "There wasn't a Nip around just then. I think his engine quit." He reached over for one of the quad maps we wore on our knees when we flew. He jabbed at it. "Shit, it was right *there*. Right on the approach to Fourteen-Mile Strip."

"That's swampy in there," someone said.

There was a silence. Airedale had another swig from the bottle, then passed it around. Those who weren't flying had a swallow. Badger, who was flying, had one too. Pretty soon Airedale left to see the medics. Everyone yelled after him that it was good to have him home. Kev walked over to the Victrola and wound up "San Antonio Rose."

Python never came back. No one ever found a sign of him or his plane.

Steve had been flying Number Two in Yellow Flight during

the Big Scramble, as we were calling it. He had been shaken when Airedale had gone missing from the flight, and was happy that he was back. "He's a pretty good old guy," he said that night in the tent. "Anyway, do you realize how it affects the odds? We had twenty people in that soiree and only lost one. That's only five percent. We should be able to take ten percent loss, they say, without any sweat."

"Yeah, but we lost four ships." I said, "That's twenty percent."

"But it's the men that count."

"Sure, but all three of us who got back were just lucky. We didn't *know* anything or *do* anything to survive. Except maybe Balz. He really worked at it with that nice little bailout."

"You worked at it, too. You got the ship back and walked away."

"Steve, I didn't do anything. I just sat there with my thumb in my ass, letting it all happen to me."

This was so palpably true that Steve was quiet for a moment. Then he brightened. "Anyway," he said. "The law of averages is way over on your side now. You've already been shot down. It's not likely to happen again."

I felt a flush of warm affection for Steve and I didn't bother to answer. Down deep, I felt that my getting shot down again *was* apt to happen, but the hell with it.

All of us were constantly analyzing disasters to see exactly where a pilot had gone wrong. There had to be a logical reason for a man to get burned in combat or a plane to spin in—some error somewhere—and we were always searching them out in our heads and sometimes in our conversation.

So, as I lay in my cot that night, under the mosquito bar, I thought about Airedale and Python. I never would have gone tear-assing off alone after a Nip as Airedale had done—yet

Airedale had come home. On the other hand, I most certainly would have bailed out as Python and Balz had done under the same conditions—yet only one of them had come home. That seemed to give me a fifty percent chance, and I didn't like it.

Uneasily, I went to sleep.

XI

Dobo

As a gesture of revenge for the big Japanese raid on Moresby, a scraping of B-17s was sent off to strike at the enemy bases on the north coast of New Guinea—Lae, Madang, Finschafen, and stops between. Long-range fighters were needed as escorts, and the 'Cobra had a short range, a blessing I suddenly appreciated. Madam Squadron with its P-38s would do most of this job, and Binky Squadron—P-40s from Dobodura, across the Owen Stanleys from Moresby—would take over Madam's

104

original mission of covering biscuit bombers near Salamaua. That left Dobodura unprotected, so Gopher was ordered to cross the mountains and spend two nights, making the region safe for democracy.

The strip at Dobo had been hacked out of the rain forest as though by a giant lawn mower. We skimmed down onto it and taxied into the cool shade of the trees to park the planes. Among the Binky people who were off duty that day was Crandall, whom Steve and I hadn't seen since flying school. He took us in tow to show us around, and he said the P-40s were just as hard to land as ever, and that he'd developed a new set of thigh muscles from kicking the rudder bar to keep from ground-looping. He said the worst thing about them was that they wouldn't wear out. "I don't know when we'll ever get new ships," he said. "These buckets just keep going."

We had only a small drink with Crandall because we would be flying in the morning. Then we went to the mess tent and were pleased to note that Binky's chow was no better than ours. Afterward we sat in their officers' tent, which wasn't nearly as nice as our farmhouse, back over the mountains. It didn't have a decent bar. It did, however, have a Dear John board where people pinned up their Dear John letters for everyone to share. A new one had just been tacked up, and Crandall paused to read it. "Dear Everett, I know that this is going to hurt you terribly, and I don't know how to 'soften the blow' very much. You mean such a lot to me, and you always will. Something 'very big' has happened to me, and you have to be the 'very first one' to know . . ." And so on.

We Gopher people thought that the idea of a Dear John board was fine. "We could put one on that post to the right of the bar," Piss-Ant said. "It would look nice there."

"As long as we remember to keep changing it," Termite

added. "We don't want a lot of messy letters sticking out all over the place."

"Whoever gets the latest Dear John gets put in charge of the board," Badger said. "That'll rotate the duty."

I found myself nodding and smiling and saying, "Yeah," and "Hey, great idea," and I suddenly wondered what the hell was happening to me. But I decided that it was better to be excited about something stupid than not to be excited about anything at all. So we all planned the decor of the farmhouse like a bunch of young wives, meeting at lunch and nattering about how things were going back home.

Crandall and the other Binky people told us about their missions up on the north coast. They said that one time while they were stooging around on patrol they spotted a small flight of Zekes about three thousand feet above them. Everyone started calling them in: "Binky leader, bandits in the sun." "Binky, Binky, have you got the bandits? Eleven high; eleven high . . ." And so on. And Binky leader was saying, "OK, Binky, OK. Don't drop your tanks yet. I see them, I see them."

And a new voice came into the headsets at that moment: "We see you, too, Binky."

Then Badger and Piss-Ant reminisced about the time when the Japanese made one of their big Moresby raids—months before my debut—and one of Gopher's new pilots got a Zeke on his tail and couldn't shake him off no matter what he did. Finally in desperation he called the Moresby sector: "Mary, Mary from Gopher White Four; I have a bandit and will bring him directly over Seven-Mile Strip. Please alert the ack-ack." And Mary came back at him, formally as ever: "Gopher White Four from Mary, please explain statement you have a bandit. Are you in pursuit?" And our guy answered, "Mary, this is Gopher White Four. Negative, negative. Bandit is in pursuit." So Mary

acknowledged that and said the ack-ack was informed, and
Gopher White Four came ripping over Seven-Mile Strip with a
hot-pants Nip right in his hip pocket. And the ack-ack opened
up—and shot down Gopher White Four. The new pilot was able
to bail out, but he was damaged a bit and sent home. He was
awfully mad, Piss-Ant said.

Then the Binky guys got talking about how during the Buna
campaign the Zeros would come off the strip to meet the P-40s.
"They took off and pulled straight up, hanging on their props,
and when they were up to two thousand feet, where we were,
they'd Immelmann out of their loop and start shooting. They
just barely had the wheels retracted."

Then the Gophers started remembering old flying characters
like Red Ned Riegle, the Australian Hurricane ace who came
back home after the Battle of Britain to help organize the RAAF
fighters. He liked to play poker with the Americans at Moresby,
but he'd get upset if he had a string of bad cards. He'd be playing down on the flight line at some squadron's alert shack, and
after a few bad hands he'd excuse himself and slip out to slow-
time a plane—that meant putting some time on a new or recon-
ditioned engine without running up the rpms too much. It was
always an excuse for a man to go up alone, for once, and play
in the sky. Red Ned would disappear, and then you'd hear the
sound of his takeoff, and then the poker game would go on
peacefully until someone would look out the open side of the
shack and say, "Oh, God, here he comes!" Red Ned's plane
would be coming straight at the shack, so low that it was actually below the level of the roof. It would be perfectly silent
because its engine noise hadn't arrived yet—you would just see
the spinner coming at you and getting bigger. And at the last
moment he would pull up to barely miss the roof, and then
WRRRAAAAAAMMM— The poker players would try to hold

down their cards and winnings, but the prop wash would come through the shack like a tornado, sending aces and ten-pound notes flying. The Gopher people said it was amazing how low Red Ned could get in an airplane if he had been losing a lot.

Then the Binky people remembered one of their old guys who had finally been sent home: Fred I-Had-A-Little-Trouble-Today McCall. They said he was a real Jonah. About once every six weeks he'd go off with his P-40 flight, and the people on the ground would see his plane start to fall behind, and hold straight instead of making the first turn to close formation. They'd watch it wobbling and sagging down behind the trees, and then way off the end of the strip they'd see a great black column of smoke going up. Everyone would shake his head sadly and say, "Jesus, poor old McCall," and word would spread around the camp that McCall had bought it. And about forty-five minutes later, into the alert shack would walk McCall, all covered with mud and scratched by thorns. He'd go up to the operations officer and lean wearily on his desk and say, "Listen, John, I had a little trouble today."

We got talking about the future. We figured the war would go on until close to 1950; "Golden Gate in '48" was considered an optimistic prediction. We thought there would be a business boom, that the Depression was finally over and that anyone who didn't get into the stock market was a fool. We thought the Zionists would set up their own nation in Palestine, and two of the Jewish guys agreed that they wouldn't mind flying for them because they would probably have to fight a bunch of Arabs. We thought it might be a good deal to stay in the service after the war because there would certainly be a separate air force and it would certainly be involved in trying to reach the moon. We felt that we ought to be able to get someone on the moon in the late 1960s. We were also quite sure that by then the president would very likely be a black lady. We foresaw a curb on population, but not a limit on power.

Next morning, we got up early to preflight our planes. The Binky mechanics were P-40 specialists, and we hadn't brought our own crew chiefs, so we went through the routine ourselves. I walked out to Nanette in the early morning starlight, running my hand along the leading edge of the wing. The dew was clean and cool, and I felt as though I were awakening her. I turned the big propeller over four times by hand to spread the oil through the twelve cylinders, then I opened the cockpit door and climbed in, switching on the light and then the other switches. Her energizer sang its rising nasal song as I heeled, then the note descended into the gulp and grind of the engager. Two shots of prime against the early morning chill, and Nanette flamed briefly from her stacks, then shuddered, barked and effortlessly rippled into action, engine purring, prop wash beating back against the door. I throttled back to let the oil warm so that the pressure would drop. Around me in the darkness I could see flashes of flame as other Gopher planes came to life. The sky was red in the east above the line of jungle, and as though to meet its coming heat, Nanette's temperature crept up and her oil pressure slid down. I could almost sense the relief in her as the tension in her cylinders eased with the flowing warmth of the explosions. I checked the radio and the switches and finally when the oil was well in the green I ran her up, thundering and quivering, and checked the mags and pitch. By the time I shut her down, she was eager and ready and so pretty as the sunrise touched her gently curved nose. I stroked it as I walked away to get breakfast, and the skin was warm and alive even that far from the engine.

We flew a couple of easy missions, enjoying the new scenery of the north coast, the clean, curved beaches, the cobalt blue water, the mountains to the left this time, their crags and precipitous slopes etched by the low sun. Nanette was beautiful, swinging gracefully from side to side as we interwove our flights on patrol. At the end of the afternoon mission, we rat-raced through the clouds that had built up and she danced and frolicked superbly, leading me on to fresh delights. As the squadron strung out into line astern to swoop and soar and wheel through the cumulus, we achieved a whiplash effect so that the last planes cut exaggerated figures as they followed the leader. Nanette and I were in the last flight, and when the leader turned gently to slide down a winding cloud corridor, we stood hard upon a wing tip and shaved the wall of mist. But she made it effortless, following every sideways rock of my trussed body, every half-muttered cry of excitement. And at the end we slow-rolled, and she laid her nose on a mountain peak forty miles away and turned on it as precisely as though she were drilling a hole in the scenery with her hard little cannon.

Back on the ground at Dobo, we found two P-38s parked near the alert shack. They had dropped in to refuel and since there was rain over the mountains they had decided not to return to Moresby until morning. One of the pilots was Guppy.

We had not kept in very close touch with Guppy since he had been sent off to Madam Squadron to learn to fly P-38s. He had dropped in a couple of times to tell us how much he liked them. This time Steve and I greeted him with a certain awe because we'd heard he had downed an enemy plane during the big raid.

"Didja really get one, Guppy?" Steve asked.

"I got one."

"You Goddamn butcher."

We learned that he had flown blindly along beside his flight leader, scared senseless, and had suddenly seen a small, brightly colored plane, much daintier and prettier than anything he had seen before, right in front of him. He had pressed his trigger convulsively, and it had blown up with a great flash.

"Are you sure it was a Nip?" I asked.

"Of course I'm not sure," Guppy said. "I haven't been sure of anything since I got to this terrible place."

He said his flight leader seemed to think he had done well, so he guessed it really was a Nip.

"How did it feel to do it?" I asked.

"I shook a lot when we got back on the ground."

Guppy said he liked flying the Lightnings, but that he didn't like exchanging shots with other planes; it seemed to him insanely dangerous. He had made up his mind to get sent home somehow. He hadn't figured out the way, but he would.

Next morning we flew another mission, very short, no problems, then returned to Dobo to refuel for the flight home to Moresby. Guppy had gone; Crandall and our Binky friends were off on a mission; we were no longer needed. And strangely, I think all of us were sort of anxious to get back to our own place, to tall, skinny Jim with his droopy mustache and his air of weary solicitude; to short, chunky Kev, the Grandpaw Pettibone of the squadron, with his inevitable cigar, his impatience with stupidity whether from a shiny new pilot or General George Kenney.

Taxiing out to take off for home, I ran Nanette through a small, gleaming puddle of what I presumed was rain water. The prop wash picked it up and sprayed it back, and I smelled something familiar, even nostalgic. I couldn't place it.

We flew back across the mountains, and Badger led us straight through a small notch in the summit line which we called the Gunsight. On the Moresby side, the range fell away like a cliff face, and as we howled through the Gunsight in tight formation, the shearing downward current made the planes drop with a hard little jar. We kept tightly together and held our noses down so that we roared over the strip going like the hammers of hell, and then we peeled up, snapped the toggle switches and settled down toward the matting, engines gurgling and belching, wheel struts moaning.

I waved at John as he guided me into my revetment, then I got out and stretched and fumbled for a damp cigarette. John was staring up at the underside of the nose section.

"Jesus, John," I said. "What's she done now?"

"She's gone and got tar on her somehow, Lieutenant," he said.

So I had to tell Kev. And Kev looked at me and shook his head.

"You've got a day off tomorrow, Park," he said. "And you know just how to spend it, don't you?"

All the next day I struggled with brushes and rags and gasoline and steel wool. John finally yielded to his natural kindness and joined in. But neither of us could get all the tar off. Nanette wore a funny little stain under her nose for the rest of her days. And I never saw it without remembering that tiny interlude at Dobo when we had been almost like barnstormers in the old days of flight. We'd had no crew chiefs, no strict operations control. We'd put our ships to bed at night and roused them at dawn, and we'd flown wonderfully informal missions: "Hey, you guys, let's wheel up the coast to around *here* and horse around for a while and then wheel on home again, OK?"

I felt I would have liked that life with Nanette.

XII

Tsili

I got back from a ten-day leave to find the squadron alive with excitement. We were going to move, it turned out. The news had been broken to us in deepest secrecy, and extraordinary precautions had been taken to keep us from spilling the beans—censorship of mail tightened, all leaves cancelled. Only the officers and a few key noncoms had ever been told.

And then, apparently, Tokyo Rose had played a selection of Glenn Miller and dedicated it "to those brave and lonesome men of Gopher Squadron, now at Port Moresby, wishing they were back with their sweethearts in the good old U.S.A.''

Of course she had everyone's attention by then, and apparently the bar at the farmhouse was so quiet you could hear the rye aging. ''These poor fellows,'' she had continued, ''will be making a move to Marilinen, far off in mountain valley, next Tuesday. We will greet them warmly—so warmly, in fact, that none of Gopher Squadron will ever be seen again.''

I heard the whole story from Steve. ''We put off the move until Wednesday,'' he said. ''Just to prove her wrong about something. Oh, and we've adopted the alternate name for the valley—the native name.''

''What is it?''

''Are you a spy? If not, it's Tsili-Tsili,''—he sounded it out carefully—''pronounced 'Silly-Silly.' ''

''What's the place like?''

''I've been over it once, escorting airborne engineers. They're putting in two dirt strips, crossing each other, with these dinky little bulldozers and graders—tiny little things they dropped in by parachute. They look like the things kids play with in sandboxes. Anyway, it's just a mountain valley with scars running across it. You'll probably see it tomorrow. How was leave? Didja get any?''

Nanette was glad to see me when I dropped around to the flight line next day to look her over and give John his bottle. She was clean and shiny on the outside—except for the ridiculous smirk caused by the tar stain—but I was shocked to smell stale cigar in her cockpit. Kev smoked cigars when he flew. A lot of us were quite certain that he would eventually blow up, lighting one in a P-39, but since he'd been flying when we were just getting into long pants, we felt a little abashed about pointing it out to him.

"Did Kev fly her?" I asked John.

He nodded. "Kev and Rabbit and Badger," he said. "They all flew her once because she's rated as a flight leader's plane. They all hated her guts, too. Kev said she was dangerous, and Rabbit said he couldn't get her up to altitude on a scramble, and Badger said she was a whore and had tried to kill him four times in two hours."

I felt very happy. I tweaked her on the pitot tube as I walked back to the jeep.

"Thanks for the bottle," John called after me. "Just the right stuff. You flying tomorrow?"

"Probably," I said.

"She'll get you up there," he said.

I did fly her, and the mission was to Tsili to cover the airborne engineers in the C-47s. Nanette hated every second of it. I coddled her over the mountains and nursed her around the area in wide circles while the transports did their stuff, and then we covered them back home and Nanette was jerky and rough and uncooperative. Her engine sounded very bad—rough, although the mags checked out OK—and she didn't want to frolic, just to drive resentfully home. We left each other in a bad temper. I kicked her left tire, and she burned my shoulder with one of her hot exhaust stacks.

That evening we got another message from Tokyo Rose. "Those tricky heroes of Gopher Squadron, down at Port Moresby, have changed the date of their move until Wednesday. They've changed the name of their new base, too. But it doesn't really matter. You're all going to buy the farm, fellows, so just relax and enjoy this nice number from Harry James. It's one your wives are dancing to, right now, with all those other boys next door."

In the general hilarity that followed, I found myself drinking with my old nemesis, Badger. I wasn't posted to fly the next day, so I climbed up the hill to my tent, past the squadron Victory garden with its fat tomatoes, and burrowed in my parachute bag for my last bottle of Scotch, now half-gone. I brought it back to the farmhouse, and because it was a nice night, Badger and I shinnied up to the roof and sat on the ridgepole, finishing it off after the rest had gone to their sacks. It turned out that Badger had been an English major at Minnesota and could recite scads of nineteenth-century poetry, from Wordsworth to Matthew Arnold.

The next time I did fly, two days later, Nanette behaved even worse than before. The pressure was on to finish the base at Tsili, for the C-47s were parading up there with a flight every two hours or so. Consequently, we split the squadron into two escort units, Number One and Number Two, of two flights each. Nanette and I were with Number One, and made two missions. On the first, she was skittish, but more or less tractable. On the second, she was simply bitchy.

Notably, she gulped gasoline as though it were going out of style. I went through the belly tank far too soon and watched the gauges drop on the main tanks while we were over the target. Finally I had to lean the mixture, and of course Nanette complained about that, detonating and overheating and losing power.

The transports seemed to take forever to slip down between those wild little hills to the scarred valley which would be our home. The day was very clear and obviously hot. Thermals from the tall kunai grass of the open lands below reached all the way up to us and we rode the great invisible heat bubbles restlessly, twitching and wavering, suddenly getting a great boot in the tail that gained us 100 feet and then just as abruptly losing it again, our stomachs lagging a half-second behind.

By the time the bus drivers had got turned around and we could head for the barn, we were all angry and tired and half-sick. I swore nastily at Nanette and she rocked so violently that I banged my burned shoulder on her door.

The C-47s poured on coal as we left the hills, and I had to rich up the mixture a bit to keep in place. My gauges were too low—I checked them with Skunk-Ass, who was leading—but no longer way too low. If everything worked out OK, I'd make it home without too much sweat. We passed the Number Two unit with their flock of transports, and waggled wings at them. They had the last mission of the day. We would be all through, thank God, as soon as we landed.

About fifteen minutes later, just as Number Two would have been reaching the target, we began picking up those unmistakable noises in our earphones that meant enemy contact. We heard voices in half-sentences—"Two o'clock level . . ." "No you don't, shit-head!" "Behind you, John . . ."—and plaintively from the transport leader, "Gopher from Whisky, what do you want us to *do?*"

Skunk-Ass spoke quickly to us: "Gopher One, anybody got enough fuel to go help out?"

No one said anything, so Nanette coughed horridly, and I said, "I don't, Skunk-Ass." Nanette smoothed out.

He said, "I know you don't, Park. Anyone else?"

Lombardi said, "I don't think I can." He was a new guy flying on my wing. Attrition was so great and squadron judgment so bad that I had been entrusted to lead an element—the last two planes of Red Flight.

Airedale then spoke up. He was leading Yellow Flight, having returned from his leave, fat and happy. "No use, Red leader," he said. "They got this one all to themselves."

I was struck by what a decent person Airedale was, a man of

consideration and politesse and above all, sound judgment. Silently we flew home, the explosive bits of talk from the combat behind us fading away with the miles. It wasn't until we had pulled together for the sweep down the strip, eight planes in tight echelon, fifteen feet off the matting, that I became aware of how smoothly and nicely my little whore was running, purring along as effortlessly as a sewing machine, steady and sweet under me, rocking out and up with a clean, crisp swing that left a pair of wing-tip contrails perfectly arced, as though drawn by an artist.

I landed and taxied to John, standing with the sun gleaming on his bare, mahogany shoulders, arms raised. He conducted me into place, cut me, and hopped on the wing to open the door.

"You looked good," he said. "How did she go?"

I started to try to tell him: She had been fine at the end of the mission, awful during the guts of it. She had been largely responsible for preventing us from going back to help out Number Two unit. She had thereby quite possibly delayed the grand final triumph of the forces of freedom over the minions of slavery, an event which already seemed distant enough. Yet once again she had saved my poor helpless ass, which was really the most overpoweringly important thing she could do. I looked at John in despair. "How did she go?" I repeated. *"I don't know."*

Of course we were all outside waiting for Number Two to get back, and when they came over the strip we noticed two things right away. There were only six of them instead of eight. They made a funny whistling noise which came from the fact that the tapes over their gun muzzles had been shot away. The sound always meant that the wing guns had been used, and that meant combat. We never shot the wing guns to clear them as we did the cannon, so they stayed taped up to prevent rust until a live target came along.

The six planes roared over us, then two broke away, circled and came back low, both rolling, one after the other. "Two victory rolls," Skunk-Ass said. "The first one's Termite—see that camouflage?—but who's the other?"

"I think it's Carter," Lombardi said. Carter had joined with Lombardi and another guy named Morgan.

"Gee, maybe it is," Airedale said. This was only about the fourth mission Carter had flown. To get a victory would be going some.

The two planes peeled up and landed and the others came in after them. Termite taxied past, grinning joyfully and holding up a forefinger to indicate one plane. The other winner was indeed Carter. He simply looked ahead intently. He was a languid, almost effeminate youngster, nearly too tall to be a fighter pilot, rather stooped, with lank blond hair and rather bulging blue eyes. He came from California, as we all later learned.

The planes came in and the pilots got into the jeeps that Elkhart and the operations clerk drove out to the revetments. We greeted them anxiously as they reached the alert shack—Jim, Steve (thank God), Morgan . . . but where was Balz? And what about Kev, for God's sake? Hadn't Kev decided to fly with Number Two on that mission? As operations officer he could fly whenever and whatever he damned pleased. Hadn't he mentioned that he'd tag along with his old friend, Jim?

Yes. Kev had gone along and the Nips had bounced them—right out of the sun—about eighteen Zekes and Oscars and a flight of nine Sally bombers. It had been a wild soiree, with planes all over the sky and the transports scuttling for the ground. Termite had caught a Zeke with a single long burst and he'd gone straight in. Balz had chased a Sally, apparently, and been caught from behind. Jim had seen him bail out and had kept an Oscar from shooting him in his chute. Steve had blasted away at a Sally and got an engine smoking.

Carter, whom no one knew very well, had shot down two Zekes and a Sally. One of the Zeke pilots had bailed out and Carter had killed him in his chute.

Kev had been the first man hit. Good old Kev, who had once flown P-26s and who smoked cigars in the cockpit so we thought he might blow up some day. He blew up anyway.

Balz landed on a tabletop mountain, collapsed his chute quickly, hid it so the Zeros wouldn't see it and strafe, and then recalled Rule One for bailouts: Sit down and think things over before you make a move. He sat down in the warm sun of a clearing near the cliff face of the mesa. He lit a cigarette and stretched and unzipped his flying suit to let the sweat dry, and he began to relax and stop shaking. And then he gradually became certain that he was being watched. Cautiously easing his gun out of its holster, he peered into the surrounding undergrowth. He saw nothing move, but the feeling was strong that someone was looking him over very carefully. Something told him to move slowly and act unconcerned, so he started to whistle a nice slow tune: "When This Bleeding War Is Over," which is the same tune as "What a Friend We Have in Jesus." Balz was aware of this, and felt that any little thing might help.

The leaves parted in eighteen different places, and Balz found he had an audience of four-foot natives—the tallest was four feet, that is. They stared at him with what appeared to be a mixture of fear and fascination, and Balz, figuring that a smile is good in any language, put on a big happy, personality-kid grin and held his hands open to show he wasn't carrying a spear—

which his little friends were. He kept his gun between his knees.

It worked. They smiled back, and then came to look him over, feeling his genitals to see what sex he was under all that silly clothing. Pretty soon he had taught one to whistle and another to smoke cigarettes and they offered him some food which he hoped wasn't person, because Balz can't stand eating person.

Anyway, in no time he got across to them that he'd like to get off the mountain. He knew he was right near Tsili with all the airborne engineers working on it and that if he used his escape compass properly he should be OK once he got down. The natives seemed to understand what he wanted and were agreeable about it—probably because they were afraid of all he would eat, he being bigger. But they had to get their wives and children first to come and stare at him. Then, when he made restless motions to get started, the headman showed him a trail, and down he went. He looked back and saw them quietly watching him go—one smoking a cigarette and another whistling.

About two months later, long after Balz had rejoined us and we had forgotten his escapade, a C-47 pulled into our revetment area and a middle-aged, bespectacled man with no hat and a lot of sudden sunburn got out and asked if there was a Lieutenant Balz hereabouts. He turned out to be an anthropology professor from one of the Australian universities and he talked to Balz for quite a while, taking notes. Balz said he was a nice man. He said that apparently these pygmies he had met were a pretty rare group of mountain people—very shy and hard to study. The professor told Balz that he had done something of real value, getting to know them a little, and Balz was very pleased.

By then, we were well established at Tsili, having made our

move right on schedule. Our camp was set up in the jungle, the tents raised among great trees that towered far overhead and left us in twilight all day long. The shade was welcome, but the air dripped moisture and the paths that led us to the mess tent were damp and black as though they were small roads to damnation.

Steve and I set up a tent, and on the second night I found a small snake in my sleeping bag. Fortunately I had not crawled in. It went away, and I went to Rabbit's tent and drank some of his whiskey because Steve and I were out. Rabbit said he'd found a scorpion in his boots that morning.

On the third day, the enemy bombed us. I was not flying and had gone to the little stream that ran by the campsite to wash myself and my clothes. I didn't hear the planes because the water was chuckling over rocks. But I did hear a strange echoing whisper, high in the air, and there was something so compelling about the sound that I ran to the bank of the stream and threw myself flat on the ground, naked. The whisper grew louder, almost as though a train were coming down the track, and then there were some grand explosions and the ground shook under me and I tried to pull myself into the soil with my fingers. I opened an eye after a moment, and stared at the grass an inch or so away. One blade had an ant on it, going about his business.

They didn't hit anything particular, and no one was hurt. But we tightened our patrols, and then they started bombing us at night. They didn't hit anything then, either, but we got very quick about diving for the slit trenches that were now being dug beside every tent. We would joke about So-and-So being the first man, invariably, to get in. "Don't jump into your trench when the shit hits the fan," we'd say to each other. "Step in carefully. Otherwise you'll hurt old So-and-So."

Badger said he was going to fly a night patrol and see if he could get one of the bombers. We all told him he was crazy. Jim said he shouldn't do it alone, but Badger said Kev would have been the only guy who could have gone with him. "None of the rest of these guys can fly at night."

Since this was perfectly true, Jim didn't argue. So Badger would go howling off at about ten o'clock and then come in a couple of hours later. He'd refuel and go up again. He covered about three-quarters of the night, three nights in a row, and then the Nips came over and we heard him chase them around (while we were sitting in the slit trenches on top of old So-and-So), and then he came back in and landed and drove back to camp.

"I couldn't see a damn thing," he said. "Somebody gimme a bottle."

The night bombing went on sporadically after that, but only Jerry's laundry got hit, and Jerry wasn't there. We would have missed Jerry if he had been there. He was a "Boong," as we called them—a Papuan—and he had been brought up in a mission so spoke perfect English. When I first joined the squadron I brought him my laundry and tried out some of the Pidgin English we had been taught. "Hey, boy," I said. "You washim lap-lap belong mefellah?"

"OK, Lieutenant," he said. "Just put it there beside the tree."

I wasn't the only one he fooled. Steve was determined to try out his Pidgin, too, and when a fighter from Madam Squadron was being "slow-timed" over our Moresby base he pointed it out to Jerry, who was nearby: "Hey Jerry, you lookim lik lik balus."

Jerry glanced up at the plane as it was whining through some acrobatics, far overhead. "Yeah," he said. "That's Colonel Scholl from Group. Man, he's shore wringin' out that 38!"

Jerry moved with us to Tsili, boiling pot, Texas accent and

all, and hated the dark forest until he found his old friend (known as Snowball in those innocently racist days) who was laundry boy for another crowd at the other end of the area. The two of them would meet for a "sing sing"—they sang hymns which had been taught them by Seventh Day Adventists—and when it was Jerry's turn to visit Snowball he'd pedal over on his bike. He'd brought it up from Moresby—it and his parasol.

We would often pass him in the jeep from the flight line—the last afternoon patrol sprawled sweatily over the hood—and Jerry would swerve his bike out of the muddy ruts to let us past. He always carried the parasol with him, and he'd slide off the bike, clutching the parasol, and come to attention and give us a British Empire salute, eyes to the front, and shout, "Hurrah!"

We loved Jerry and knew that some day, if we started to win the war and had to move north into Dutch New Guinea, we'd lose him. Those were the days of unwitting racial cruelties—we laughed at nigger jokes and took for granted that the Pullman porter was black and woolly-headed and amusing. But we were also bright, more or less educated young men and we often winced at injustices that we saw and argued about what the future would bring to the Negroes ("Blacks" was a word we never thought of using). We weren't much concerned. What the hell—we'd just barely discovered the Jews and we thought of women with a mixture of adoration, condescension, and lust. The way we saw it, Bojangles was still tap-dancing in the kitchen while Shirley Temple went down the street to make friends with the Cohens.

We flew short missions out of Tsili-Tsili because we were very close to the land fighting, where the Australians were bashing away at the Japanese. We would fly overhead while C-47s dropped supplies to the diggers, and sometimes we would be low enough to see figures dashing out to get the boxes and bales that had tumbled from the transports. Often we were asked to strafe a certain area. We would gather in our alert tent and look at Elkhart's big map. He would show us where the enemy positions were and where the Australians were—a thick red line marked the difference. But it was on the map, not on the rain forest, and when we went over the trees, dodging through the hills, we just shot and shot at the jungle until we saw big fellows, stripped to the waist, waving broad-brimmed hats at us. Then we would stop shooting and all of us would do a slow roll, and the diggers would all come out of their foxholes and wave.

We always asked if we'd hit any of them by mistake, and Elkhart would say not to worry about it—it would only be a few, and we were really messing up the Nips.

That Christmas we got a card from the Australian Seventh Division wishing us all the best and thanking us for a superb strafing job on November 19. None of us could remember what we had done on November 19. We had shot up a lot of jungle, that was all, just as we did almost every day.

One evening we were asked to do some dive bombing. The planes were fitted with 500-pound bombs instead of belly tanks, and we gathered around Jim and Rabbit, who had been made operations officer to take Kev's place. "Has anyone done any dive-bombing?" Jim asked. There was a silence until someone pointed out that he'd seen a movie once with James Cagney and Pat O'Brien, and it was about navy dive-bombing, and they went almost straight down, using the gunsight on the target, and then released just as they pulled out. Jim and Rabbit were very interested.

"We can't go straight down like that," Jim said. "These ships would just plow into the hills."

"That means we'll have to use deflection on the gunsight," Rabbit said. "We'll lay off a few rads to make up for going in on a slant."

"How high should we pull out?" someone asked.

"Well," Jim said, "at that altitude the planes will mush when we pull out. We'd better allow 500 feet."

"In all those navy movies, the dive bombers do a wingover when they get to the target," Steve said. "And aren't they always in echelon until they peel off?"

"Yeah," someone said, "and they all have white scarves . . ."

"And Cagney is the fourth man to go in," someone else said, "and he's pissed off at Robert Taylor—"

"—for making time with his girl—"

"—Priscilla Lane."

"Shut up," said Jim, affably. "If we go into the target in echelon, we'll be able to make our dives from constantly changing angles. That makes sense, because it will allow us to see each other. Also, if there's any flak . . ."

"Flak?" I asked, nervously.

"No flak," Elkhart put in quickly. "The Australians say it's a field-gun battery—not antiaircraft."

"OK, then," Jim said. "I'll lead you over in this direction"—he showed us on the map—"and we go into echelon and circle the target this way and then peel off, one after the other. The bombs are set for a delay, so we should all be out of the way before the first one goes off. Dive as steeply as you can in those hills, but allow that 500 feet to haul out. Lay your gunsights on the target and then raise it about—what do you think, Rabbit, four rads?—I guess about four rads, and then release and haul ass. Got it?"

Thus imperfectly we taught ourselves to dive-bomb. That first attempt was beautiful. The air was still and sweet over the hills, and the sun was low so that contours stood out clearly below us, etched against their shadows. We formed a neat, straight echelon, circling gently until Jim called us. "See that little round hill in the valley? See the big tree on top of it?"

Someone else broke in, excitedly, "It looks like a tit with a nipple."

"That's it," Jim said. "If anyone hasn't got it, watch me," and down he went.

With a joyous whoop, on the radio, the next pilot peeled off, and then the next shouted, "Geronimo!" and went down, and everyone yelled something. It was absolutely glorious fun, and Nanette loved it. She had always enjoyed low-level work as long as there was no opposition, and this time she was at her best, in conditions that thoroughly suited her—glassy air, no shooting back, no way to see what we were hitting, if anything, a steep dive and a flashy pullout and lots of whooping and yelling on the radio. In all, a riotous party.

We pitched over on the left wing and I eased her nose onto that nipple and raised it and yanked the release and up she went, reaching for the tip of a great cloud in the dark blue sky. I let her soar on up, increasing pressure gently until she was on her back, and then we rolled out in an Immelmann and were left hanging almost stalled out on top of 2,000 feet of air, delighted with each other. For a moment, there wasn't a sign of another plane, and even the earphones were still.

"Alone at last," I said into my oxygen mask, and I heard her chuckle.

We formed up and flew home and landed and all of us were so pleased with ourselves that we just sat around the alert tent, talking and laughing until Elkhart pointed out that chow would be ready soon and if we wanted a drink beforehand we'd better get back to camp.

No one knew whether we'd hit anything until the next night when Jim came into the pilot's tent after supper, waving a piece of paper. It was from a lieutenant colonel in command of the second something-or-other brigade, Seventh Division, Australian Imperial Force, and it said, "Gopher Squadron bloody marvelous. One case whiskey en route with our thanks." I think perhaps it was our finest hour.

Time passed at Tsili. Jim got orders to go home and we all got very drunk and Steve threw up. Rabbit was made CO. Badger had taken Kev's place as operations officer and flew in any flight he wanted. The Fifth Air Force even sank so low as to make me a flight leader and assign me a plane, all to myself. I knew it would be Nanette, because I had been almost the only pilot who flew her. As Jim had once said, nobody else could stand her. After I read the orders I went down to the flight line in a flight leader's jeep, and walked around her. I wondered if I should have her name painted on the door: "Nanette" in fat curved lettering, with a Disney-type cartoon of—of what? A pussycat?

I looked at her, clean and shiny with her worn olive drab paint and her smirk of tar like badly applied lipstick. She was an airplane, that's what she was, not some damn animal.

So Nanette never did have her name painted on her. John stenciled mine and his on opposite sides of the cockpit, as was customary. There was a lot of empty space nearby for Japanese flags. Oh, well.

There was no change in our relationship. I was taking my lawful wife to bed, now, instead of my mistress, but she was the same thing, and the ecstasy was the same in its sparse moments amid all the same frustrations.

Our work with the Australians on the ground developed into a career—far more enjoyable than flying high-altitude escorts, a dull and tedious job. The Royal Australian Air Force had a little two-seat training plane called a Wirraway, almost exactly like the AT-6 that we had used in advance school. The Aussies used these in what they called their army cooperation squadrons, for spotting and strafing enemy positions. We would sometimes see the Wirraways—there were always two of them—chugging off into the mountains to search out some bunker that was giving the diggers trouble. The rear gunner would be perched head and shoulders higher than the pilot and he would wave at us furiously because the Wirraway looked enough like a Nip plane to get itself shot down with some regularity. One of our new men—we had a shipment of replacements, all looking pink-cheeked and healthy and neatly uniformed and well behaved—shot down two Wirraways in a week.

Perhaps because of this, the local army co-op squadron at Tsili was given a new Australian plane called the Boomerang. This was a tiny little thing, a single-seater, very fast and maneuverable close to the ground. It had swept-back wings, so that it actually looked a little like a boomerang as you looked down on it, but that didn't deter our new man. He shot one of the first Boomers down, too, and we immediately dubbed him the Japanese Ace. Fortunately, most of the Aussie air crews managed to get out.

We were now often assigned to fly cover for the Boomerangs as they worked over the high ridges where the heavy land fighting was. We would send up a flight of four 39s and meet two Boomerangs, and they would dart around through the trees until they spotted what they were after. Then they would call us, always bursting with enthusiasm: "Gopher, Gopher, this is Duckling, here. We've got a beaut target. Watch our tracers and come on down. Right?"

The two little brown-green planes would then zing down at some patch of jungle, and we would see the red lines converge, and keep our eyes on the point while we dropped our wings and came snarling in and cut loose with the guns.

Leaves would fly, and a little dust would rise down in the underbrush, and the Australians would shout, "Whacko! Right in the bloody dial!" And then we would all flounce happily off home again.

Always, as we neared the base, the Boomerangs would drop behind us and begin shooting us down. Suddenly I would hear a voice in my earphones: *"Ba-ba-ba-ba-ba-ba-ba-ba!* Got you, 74, you're bloody dead!"* I would smack the stick froward so that all the crap in Nanette's cockpit went weightless, and we would howl for the ground, and then I'd twist up and off to the side, wrenching around to try and get a "shot" at the Boomerang. It was hard because they could turn on a dime, but we could always get away momentarily by breaking straight down.

The sky would be full of planes for a while, with people shouting *"Ba-ba-ba-ba-ba-ba-ba-ba-ba!"* at each other, just like kids with toy guns defending a city block. But when we'd edged close to the base, writhing and capering in a whirling ball of airplanes, we would pick up a call from the sector asking for identification, and we would straighten ourselves up and fly home sedately, the two Boomerangs tucked primly together like little girls going off to school, hand in hand, while the four 'Cobras slid into echelon behind and above them, acting for all the world like anxious parents.

Naturally we made friends with the RAAF boys. They would

sometimes taxi into our squadron area to check something on Elkhart's map and talk over tomorrow's mission. They'd have a drink with us before they went home. And once they asked us to their mess for dinner. They had fresh ears of corn that they'd been growing in their squadron garden. They knew Americans liked this sort of thing so they piled the table with their whole harvest. We almost cried with pleasure. They also produced plenty of good booze and a plethora of dirty songs which they willingly taught us.

The Australian ground troops that we met were another breed—rather grim professional killers. It took them a long time to laugh.

We covered the Australian landings at Finschafen, getting into the air so early that the takeoff was nearly blind, and the light was still faint when we reached the coast and looked down at the landing craft, cutting interweaving Vs in the murky water. Nanette was terribly nervous, for it seemed impossible that the Nips would let this take place go without hitting it—and that meant hitting us. But it had been so early in the morning that, I'm convinced, she never had a chance to think up a ruse which would keep us safely out of it. I know I couldn't come up with anything.

The Nips let us go for all that first day, however. And when I was assigned to lead a flight behind Badger the next day, I was quite confident that the enemy was simply going to fight this one on the ground. My Number Four man couldn't get a good mag check, so I found myself leading a three-plane flight.

Badger got bored just patrolling the combat zone, so he took us down on an impromptu strafe. We blasted away at some thatched houses which we presumed were occupied by Japanese, and we got so low that the Japanese Ace, who was flying Badger's wing, hit a coconut tree. He pulled out OK, but his plane began flying funny, and Badger told him to get home. So he did, and there was a coconut embedded in the leading edge of his wing. It had torn things up a bit.

Then my wingman called in that he was too low on fuel and would have to go back with the Japanese Ace. Steve, who was leading Badger's element, said he was way down, too. That left Badger and his wingman, wonder boy Carter, and me and my element leader, Morgan. Nanette's fuel gauges weren't exactly spilling over, but I had enough to finish the mission and get home. She was running nicely and had made a fine strafing pass—dipping her wings to wiggle between the trees, wrenching her nose down to lay her guns on whatever there was.

We had no sooner got back to altitude than there was a call from Sector warning us that bogies were on the way from the north and should be over us now. Nanette, of course, went into shock, coughing and complaining as she always did at the first hint of danger. I felt very cottony about the mouth and decided suddenly that I really didn't have gas enough for this nonsense. I was about to call Badger and break the news, when old Hawk-eye Carter, the eagerest beaver of them all, went and sighted the Nip planes.

They were coming in from the sea, a thousand feet above us, six Lily bombers and, above them, a shimmering mass of Zeros, darting and glinting all in unison like a school of little silvery fish. Nanette's engine began running so rough that I was sure it would quit. I had my thumb on the mike button when Badger cut in. " 'Come, dear children, let us away,' " he said. So what the hell was I to do with a man who gave us Matthew Arnold at a time like that? "This is it," I shouted at Nanette. "You behave or I'll kick your Goddamn rudder off!"

Well, she didn't really behave, but we stayed with Badger, climbing to intercept the Lilies. And then the four of us put our noses way up, to the point of stalling, and we all fired. We were out of range, shooting almost straight up, but I had a flash of the tracers looping almost to the bombers. The planes were creamy white in the blue sky and the meatballs were bright red. The tracers were red, too, arcing up slowly, then falling away. And beyond the six creamy bombers, farther into the blue sky, with the sun's glare behind them, the silver Zeros all flashed at once as they rolled on their backs in unison. Zeros would always do that: Shoot at them, and they'd roll upside down. Then they'd split-S down on whoever had cut loose. They were always above us, so they never just looked up when they were shot at. They looked down, rolling so the wings wouldn't block the view. They'd see our tracers go past, *whap-whap-whap,* and they'd react. Roll. Split-S. And *blam-blam-blam* right back. Now everyone knows what it was like to fight a Zero.

These flashed again, pale silvery lines against the blue, with the sun half-blurring them out. For just a moment we were all facing each other—about twelve of them heading straight down in their split-S; four of us heading straight up, standing on our tails, all stalled out. I could see the winking lights along their wings as their guns fired. And we stood up to them—even Nanette and I—and fired back.

Then, instantly, she stalled out and I kicked her nose over and we simply howled earthward, building up splendid speed. I craned around to look behind and saw the rest of the flight diving their heads off, all going in different directions. The Zeros were already giving up the chase, turning back to shepherd the bombers. It was as though the kids in a street gang had heaved a rock at a patrol car and were running for their lives down dark alleys while the cops gave chase and then disgustedly let them go. We had the same sense of immense daring that left us giggling with panic.

We all got back to base, so low on fuel we were flying on the fumes. We just slid onto the strip without peeling up, and Morgan's engine quit while he was taxiing to his revetment. The guys in the squadron came out to meet us, for our tapeless guns had whistled as we came in. We learned that sector had reported that the bombers turned away. It seemed too much to think that we had driven them away, but *post facto* there it was. We sat in the alert tent, answering Elkhart's questions and grinning at each other. Carter was not as happy as the rest of us. He was looking for his fourth victory.

Nanette had behaved beautifully. I had taken my whore to the cotillion and she had acted like a debutante. But she soon made it clear that she was never going to be put in that position again. She decided to have carburetor trouble.

The Australian landings along the coast had gone well, and again we were asked to escort Boomerangs around a mission station where the diggers were slugging it out. Rabbit led, with Morgan on his wing. I flew element with Carter on my wing. He had begged to come because he felt we would see some Zeros. It was a murky day, ominous clouds, bad visibility, the ground below looking as though Walt Disney had painted it to scare little kids. The Australians were strangely silent as they darted among the trees, looking for something. And when they called us to come down after them, they lacked their usual enthusiasm. It was just businesslike. We came in and shot and pulled back up and Nanette began to miss badly.

This was worse than her usual reluctance, and I was forced to fall back. I called Rabbit and told him, and he said OK. After all, we just had to stooge around a little longer until the Boomers had finished with their games.

The trouble was that just then the Boomers spotted some Nip planes, and we looked, and there were three of them quite low, slender and shiny against the dark clouds. We turned toward them and piled on throttle and Nanette quit cold. "Go on," I shouted at Carter, and he tore off to try another score and I was left alone.

I nursed the engine to life by throttling back. Every time I opened it up, it missed badly. Rabbit and Morgan and Carter were far ahead, tearing after the Nips who had turned away. The Australians were still calling them in, even after Rabbit called back that we saw them.

Nanette limped along after the action until I saw the other three turn back. At that point I figured the work was over anyway, so I called Rabbit and told him I was snafu. "OK," he said. "Go on ahead." The Australians kept cutting in with more calls about the Nips. We wished they'd shut up.

To get some speed, I put Nanette's nose down and we flew home low against that dismal, shadowy jungle, the clouds building above us, the darkness increasing. I felt a great sense of pressure on me, strangely, for I liked flying alone. I was very glad to see the strip wheel into place before me and feel Nanette reaching for it with her wheels. It was very good to be back.

The others came in soon after. No one had got one, though Carter was sure he'd scored hits and Rabbit thought he had, too. We were surprised to see the Boomerangs taxi up, while we were talking about it.

Their leader, a pilot officer whom we'd gotten drunk with at their mess, went over to Rabbit.

"Who was your straggler?" he asked. "Did he make it back?"

Rabbit nodded toward me. The PO looked relieved.

"It was smart of you to hit the deck that way," he said. "They lost sight of you in the dark."

"Who did?"

"The Nips, of course."

"They were miles off. We were chasing them."

"Not those; the others. We counted three flights of at least twelve each, ducking in and out of the clouds above you. We thought you were cooked."

John found that the carburetor was worth changing so he put in a new one. It seemed to check out, but while we were on a patrol we got a call from sector that a flight of bombers was coming down the Ramu Valley and would we intercept. Instantly I got the same reaction from Nanette as before—a bad engine miss as soon as I opened throttle.

I called in and Badger told me to stay where I was while the others—we had all four flights that day—climbed on up. So I circled aimlessly, humiliated and exasperated and relieved, all at once. The radar blip turned out to be a thunderstorm, so back down came the squadron, spiraling, and I turned to meet them.

A voice crackled suddenly: "Gopher leader from Gopher Blue leader, three o'clock level." And this time I was an old enough hand so I knew what he'd seen. "Blue leader," I said. "It's me! It's me!"

Badger's voice came in, a little wearily. "Don't shoot, fellows. It's only Park." And the fifteen slim noses with their round cannon muzzles swung past me. For a moment they had been aimed right down my throat.

After that Rabbit took me aside. "What the hell's wrong with your plane, anyway? That's a new carb."

"I don't know," I said. "She loses power just the way she did before."

"Look," he said. "Nothing against you, but I'm going to test-hop it. Maybe you need a leave or something."

I watched a little truculently as he jeeped over to Nanette and climbed in. It wasn't at all right to see her taxiing out with somebody else. I wondered how she would behave. If she was naughty, my reputation was saved, but if she was good I might get a leave. Reputation seemed an empty virtue at Tsili-Tsili. I prayed that she'd be good.

Rabbit was back within ten minutes. He was white and shaken. "Jesus Christ, what an airplane," he said. "That's the first time ever that a plane has quit on takeoff with me. That murdering bitch!"

So John put in another carburetor, and I didn't go on leave.

Life became easier for Nanette when Tsili was used as a forward staging base for some mighty raids on Rabaul, far to the north. Bombers went over every day with P-38s as escort (they had the range to do it) and all we did was fly local air defense. Guppy was on all the Rabaul missions. He would stop off with us to refuel, and Steve and I would try to get to see him. Usually he was off again with barely a greeting.

On the last day of the raid series he came by and this time he said he was going to spend the night. There was no flight for Madam Squadron the next day, and Guppy said he'd run out of whiskey so would it be OK if he drank some of ours?

It was, and he did. He told us that he had figured out how to get home—drink. He'd talked to the group flight surgeon, who agreed that if a pilot drank himself into oblivion every night he probably would fade some, and that group headquarters was just barely safety-conscious enough to avoid using a man who simply could no longer fly.

Since this happy revelation, Guppy had cornered all the squadron whiskey that would have been issued to the Bible-belt kids who had taken the pledge at age three. They remained clean and pure and bright-eyed and ready to die for Uncle Sam, and Guppy and a few other dissolute easterners got dirtier and dirtier and more and more red-eyed, and worse and worse in the air. At least that was the theory.

The ridiculous fact was that Guppy, in the midst of his program of self-destruction, became an ace.

"I go into combat blind with panic," he told us that night. "And I fly just as fast as I can so no one will be able to hit me. And every time I see a meatball, I shoot. And four fucking times I've hit the poor bastards and there was someone on my wing so pure and honest that he told the rest of the squadron about it afterwards." He took a huge gulp from the bottle. "Four times—plus that first one at Moresby—makes me a fucking ace. And when I see these poor, eager shit-heads wanting to fly their asses off every day and roll up big scores and wear sloppy caps on leave and pick up all the birdmen's badges in the world and smoke cigars and get interviewed on the newsreels— *you* know what I mean—" we nodded—"—they'd hack up their mothers to be me. And all I want is to go home."

He told us the Rabaul raids were so scary that he wet his pants. "The Nips put up about a hundred fighters the first day and chewed us all up, and MacArthur issued a communiqué saying Rabaul was as good as wiped out. And the next day they flung about three times as much at us, and afterwards Mac-Arthur said Rabaul was completely neutralized. And the next day the sky was so black with Nips you couldn't see the sun. That was when I met one."

Steve and I looked at him questioningly, and he went on to tell us how, in the midst of a great swirling combat, he found a Tony—the sleek little in-line engine Japanese fighter—right on his wing. Guppy looked at the Jap pilot, and the Jap looked back at Guppy. They both had oxygen masks and goggles and Guppy said the Jap wore the same kind of helmet.

They stared at each other for a moment, and then Guppy noticed the Jap beginning to fall behind, and he saw to his horror that he had cracked open his flaps so he could slide behind Guppy and clobber him. Quickly Guppy cracked open his own flaps and so managed to slow up beside the Nip, watching him all the time.

Then the Tony's underside opened up and the wheels started coming down. Back he slid, fast. So Guppy wrenched his wheel lever and the P-38 shuddered and moaned as its wheels came down, and he managed to stay with the Tony.

Guppy said he knew that any Japanese plane could hold off a stall longer than any American plane, so he guessed he had bought the farm. He said he thought about the half a bottle he had stashed away in his sack for that night and wondered who would find it and hoped it wasn't some Bible-belt kid, who would probably send it home with his effects.

With flaps and wheels down, the Tony began getting astern again, and Guppy chopped his throttle way down and just barely held even—and suddenly the sky was full of planes chasing each other and shooting and yelling on the radio so both Guppy and the Nip managed to break away without killing each other. Guppy said he hoped the Nip made it OK. He said he felt he had gotten to know him.

Guppy was fairly well ploughed by now and Steve and I wondered how he took care of his hangovers.

"I get into the cockpit of my plane early—before takeoff time—and suck oxygen," Guppy told us. "This serves several purposes: It makes me feel good; it gets rid of enough oxygen so I can snafu the mission after about two hours; it fills the rest of the squadron with a feeling of awe and respect when they see me trudging out to my plane so early every morning.

Guppy said good night, and very carefully and purposefully

made his way out into the dark, aiming for the transient tent that was set aside for visitors. We heard a splash and a muttered imprecation as he fell into our slit trench—which had rain water in it—and then there was silence and then a more distant splash and curse, and so on as Guppy the killer made his way to bed.

The weather at Tsili turned foul. For ten days in a row we couldn't get a ship off the ground, which was fine, and the C-47s couldn't get in with food, which was bad. After a week of living on peanut butter, which we had plenty of, and hard-tack, which had gone weevily so we banged each piece before eating it, we began to laugh madly at silly things—trite sayings, made-up limericks, the spectacle of two native dogs copulating.

When the weather cleared, Badger went out to his plane, started it up, and tried to taxi to the strip. A wheel sank into the deep mud and the idling propeller caught a runway marker—a small lamp—and lobbed it sixty feet in the air. It took two more days before we could fly.

The other areas apparently dried out better, though, for our food started arriving again and so did the Nip bombers. We were in and out of slit trenches a lot, and the morning when we got fresh eggs—an intricate swapping deal with the navy, too complicated to describe—a Tony strafed us at breakfast, stitching holes in the mess tent while we all instantly dove under the tables, carrying our plates of fried eggs with us.

At last we were back to normal, flying sometimes two missions a day. Lombardi, the handsomest and nicest guy in the squadron, bailed out over a lovely green valley when his engine quit. Lombardi was one of those few who are serenely truthful, getting to the marrow of truth no matter how hard to crack the calcified rumors and prejudices that envelop it. We could moan and wail about how rough things were, and Lombardi would neatly and pleasantly put us back into perspective: Would we prefer having our families mashed by bombs in their sleep, as in London? And as for discomfort, why not use the jungle instead of fearing it? Why not make bits of furniture out of the timber, fastening poles together with vines if we lacked any other way? Any fool could tie a knot. Why not hunt the wild boars that raided the native gardens? Why not learn to find the fruits and the roots that the escape manuals talked about, but that we instinctively recoiled from trying? Why not write about the life we were forced into instead of groaning about it? The guy was a survivor, and in a quiet, self-disparaging way made us all want to prosper, somehow, from our misery.

And now he was calling us with his cheerful, confident voice, saying that he'd lost all his oil pressure and was going into the red with temperature, and he guessed he'd have to get out. We all hung back beside him, watching his plane as he made his preparations—unhooking himself from oxygen, maybe tightening his parachute straps, flicking open his Sutton harness. He kept radio lines on until the end, and we all talked to him, telling him we had his coordinates, that we'd have a rescue plane there in no time, that we'd watch him down, that the valley looked like a great place and we almost envied him.

Suddenly he said, "Gopher, my engine's frozen. I'm leaving the ship."

"So long, Lombardi," we all said. "We've got you."

And we saw his plane slow way down and his door fly off. And then he came out, sprawling in the air like a spider on a web until the chute streamed from him and popped open. We circled it carefully, and saw him wave. And we saw him land in a clearing in his valley and gather in the silk and wave again.

We buzzed him, waggling our wings, and we made a careful call to sector—which had been monitoring us anyway. We had the coordinates down cold. Then we left for Tsili.

The next morning a Cub landed in the area and soon linked up with an Australian commando patrol which had managed to slip in. No one found anything. Not a sign. Nothing. We never saw Lombardi again. And we conjectured—late on a drunken evening when the flight surgeon had given us some of his alcohol and we had mixed it with melted fruit drops from a Red Cross package and had sung all our dirty songs and talked loudly and portentously about life and what purpose we served in it—we conjectured that Lombardi had set up a small kingdom in that pleasant and remote valley and was running it the way it ought to be run—with justice and honesty and courage and all the things that we knew Lombardi had in store for whoever was fortunate enough to be beside him.

XIII

Nadzab

The town of Lae is one of the chief ports of northern New Guinea, sprawled at the mouth of the broad Markham River, where it meets Huon Gulf. It had been a shipping center for Markham Valley plantations and gold mines farther inland until the Japanese invaded it and turned it into a formidable base from which to launch air attacks on Moresby. The Australian planters and miners and shopkeepers of the region either joined a strange and romantic group of irregular troops known as the

143

New Gunea Volunteer Rifles, or offered their expertise to the Allied forces gathering in northern Australia, or in a few cases stayed on within sight of their own homes and secretly radioed information about enemy movements down to the intelligence setup at Moresby.

I met an example of each of the first two categories. Steve and Guppy and I got drunk with an NGVR in a pub back in Townsville. He was a red-haired, slender man with nervous habits who vastly enjoyed his status with the other drinkers and would tell you his adventures in great detail at the slide of a bar glass. They sounded exciting, but also hopeless—a series of hairbreadth escapes in a long retreat to Moresby, during which hardly any dents were made on the Japanese.

At Charters Towers, we were taught Pidgin English by a Lae planter named Carl. He was a bluff, red-faced man with a million things to tell us, but the time to get across only a few. We learned the basic phrases that would explain to the natives the fact that you were a downed pilot ("Balus belong mefellah e buggerup finish") and that you wanted to see a "man belong Sydney" and that the natives had better play straight with you ("You gaminim mefellah' plenty trouble e come behind"). If we felt like trying some political indoctrination, we could always point out that "Japan e no good," and that "Man belong Sydney e got plenty gun." If you were picked up by mission boys, you would get red-carpet treatment by telling them that you were a "man belong Pope." They might even find some milk for you—especially if you asked for "su-su belong bulamacow."

Carl tickled us with his phrase for a piano: "Beg fella bockis e got teeth, you bangim e sing," and revealed that Pidgin for fornication was "push-push." He said that when the Japanese invaded he made an abortive attempt to hide the family silver, but carefully and deeply buried a case of Scotch in his garden.

I never met a "coast watcher," as the informers were called. But I know that our Yellow alerts were the result of their radio calls. If a flight of enemy planes lifted off Lae airstrip, a coast watcher would send the word. They had to move frequently, and we were told that voices that had become familiar to the listeners in Moresby would suddenly no longer be heard.

MacArthur pulled off a dramatic, highly publicized attack on Lae in which paratroops jumped at the broad kunai-covered region up the Markham Valley that was called Nadzab. The newsreels ground away as MacArthur stood in the door of a C-47 watching the chutes float down on Nadzab. It was a great sight for the moms back home. The top command always thought of the moms first.

I was on leave, so missed the show. Steve told me that it was pretty good fun covering the jump—"more Goddamn planes than you ever saw in your whole life"—and Rabbit said he'd been called down to a briefing at Group just before the transports left with the paratroopers, "and there they all were, filing on board with their faces painted green." He said they carried what seemed like 200 pounds of equipment. And he said the really notable thing about them was that they were Americans. None of us had ever seen American troops in the battle zone, though a few had been used alongside the Australians when Buna was captured.

The jump went off splendidly, with only a couple of guys killed from chutes that got snarled up. There weren't any enemy troops up that valley to offer any resistance, so all that green paint and heavy equipment didn't make much difference, but it was great for the moms back in Cleveland, watching the newsreels.

While it was going on, the Australians managed to capture

Lae in a bloody bit of fighting. And as soon as the base was all cleaned up—the meat buried and the split-toed Japanese sneakers burned and the wrecked Betty bombers bulldozed off the strip—Gary Cooper came to visit the little town in order to make it clear to the world that a great bastion of Hirohito's yellow hordes had fallen and that now it was time, at last, for the battle-weary GI Joes to get what every American mom knew they needed most, some great Hollywood entertainment from Mr. Deeds himself.

We had the signal honor of putting on an air show for Cooper. Rabbit was apparently told that this might happen when he went to Moresby before the assault. And one evening he got us into the officers' tent at Tsili and told us about how Gopher Squadron had been chosen to give Gary Cooper a glimpse of American air power.

"This has got to be timed just right," Rabbit said. "Just as Cooper's transport rolls to a stop in front of the American brass, and he gets out and walks over to them, we're supposed to buzz the strip. We'll have four flights in two echelons, the second eight planes a little higher than the first eight and coming right behind them. The strip there is too narrow to get all sixteen across it, down low. At least that's what Group says."

He said he would lead in Blue Flight, and Badger would lead Red Flight, the head of the second echelon. I was to be Badger's element leader.

Rabbit didn't need to tell us that we had to do this right. We could strafe the wrong target, fail to intercept a Japanese raid, shoot down a Boomerang by mistake, or be twenty minutes late in making a rendezvous with biscuit bombers, but by God we were going to put on a hell of an air show for Gary Cooper, right at the proper second. That was important.

I felt the old adrenalin pumping as Nanette and I taxied out to takeoff. John, suitably impressed with the meaning of this mission, had gone over her carefully, replacing two spark plugs. She was running like silk and her windshield was crystal-clean.

We took off and formed up and headed off toward Lae, everyone nervously looking at the dashboard clocks, which seldom told the right time because they had to be set every time you started up. Rabbit kept us away from Lae, leading us in a broad sweep right over Salamaua. I jumped when I looked down on that old forbidden ground, but then I remembered that a couple of Australian regiments had taken it, too, as a sort of afterthought to Lae. Seen thus, it revealed itself as a pretty place, probably great fun to visit.

Huon Gulf was smooth and blue in the afternoon sun. It was a lovely day for an air show. Surely it must be time now. Nanette's clock showed about ten minutes to go. No one said anything on the radio.

I glanced at Morgan on my wing and he pointed to his wristwatch, questioningly. I made a helpless, "I don't know" gesture with my hands.

Finally, Rabbit rolled out of a wide turn, over the water, and waggled his wings. We saw Yellow Flight swing to the left of Blue, in echelon, and begin easing in close. Closer than I'd ever seen. The wing tips seemed to be tapping on the next man's door. "Boy," I said to Nanette. "Beautiful!"

Badger slid directly behind and just above Rabbit. I had been spread to the right in the usual patrol formation, so I crossed under and came up on the left, Morgan swinging from my right wing to my left. Morgan eased in so tight I could have touched his wing tip, and then I eased in on Blake, Badger's wingman, watching carefully as I fitted Nanette's wing tip right up to his door. Blake's eyes were glued on Badger. Badger was concentrating on Rabbit, right ahead of him. I could feel Morgan's eyes on me and I wondered how close he was. Quickly I stole a look and found myself staring at his wing tip. It was almost in my face. Beyond him I had a flash of four more planes in perfect alignment, barely wavering. And just ahead of us and slightly below was a ruler-set line of seven planes, slanting back and to the left of Rabbit.

What a great time to be jumped by the Nips, I thought. And I wondered if Balz, who was always a wise-ass, would suddenly call in, "Bandits, six o'clock high!" The thought made me chuckle, and to my horror Nanette joggled just slightly with my mirth. Hastily I grew properly sober and kept her smooth.

Staring at Blake, I felt the speed building up as Rabbit aimed down for the Lae strip. Faster, faster; the cockpit picking up a special note from rushing air that it always sang at about 300 miles an hour. From the corner of my eye I could see the water getting closer below and the pale coral of the Lae strip coming nearer ahead. As we settled very low over the water I sensed the slight added lift from the ground effect. But the air was so smooth we were able to hold our double rank motionless. We're not really this good, I thought to myself. But it can't last more than a few seconds longer.

Nanette gave a little jar along with the others, as we flashed over the shore. Then I had a peripheral glimpse of a silver transport right under me and figures standing by it. And then there was sky ahead as the sixteen planes eased up to clear the rain forest. Relaxing, we started to come apart a little, but Badger's voice came into the headsets.

"Hey, Rabbit, there's plenty of room for all sixteen in a line. Let's buzz 'em again after I tack on to your flights."

Old eager, at it again. Still, it had been pretty good fun, and it was a great day for it. Badger led us up next to Yellow Flight and tucked his wing into the lap of their Number Four man.

With a very gentle turn we managed to keep the tight formation—all sixteen planes now in a single echelon—and at the same time get headed back down at the strip.

Back we came in parade dress—better than the newsreels, any day. We blammed down the strip, eased up again and then suddenly I saw Rabbit haul way back and shoot for the ceiling, leaving the rest of us behind. He drew contrails from his wing tips as he kept his arc all the way onto his back. Then he Immelmanned out. By that time the radio was full of "Yippees!" and everyone was all over the sky. I don't remember what Nanette did, exactly, but I have a hazy impression of a couple of barrel rolls and then of buzzing the strip again to get a good look at Gary Cooper. I don't know if I saw him. The sky was full of Gopher planes, all about to collide, and the ground was full of brass hats, all waiting to see the collisions, and I suppose Cooper was there somewhere.

After a bit of rat-racing, we straggled back together and flew on back to Tsili, very proud of ourselves. We waited for some word from the brass: "Nice job, Gopher," or "Court martials for every pilot for dangerous flying," or "Gary Cooper loved it," or Gary Cooper hated it," or just "Wow!" We got nothing. Not a flicker of reaction. Years later I met a Hollywood flack who had been with Cooper on that junket and remembered landing at Lae.

"I was right over your head," I shouted at him excitedly. "I was in the air show they put on for him."

"What air show?" he asked, puzzled. "There were some planes around. Was that an air show?"

"Listen," I said, "were the planes very low? Were they in a slanty line, sort of bunched together? Close?"

"Yeah, I guess so," he said. "There was a lot of noise. No one could hear Coop's speech."

"Well, didn't he stop and watch the planes?"

"I don't know. I didn't notice. Usually he just got through what he had to do. He was a real sweetheart, Coop was."

After a while, when the strips were built at Nadzab, we moved there. We said good-by to our funny little jungle camp at Tsili and put up our tents in the kunai grass. It was dryer than the jungle, but blistering hot compared to the damp shade we were used to. We learned to hang supply parachutes inside these pyramid tents, providing a false ceiling where the hot air was trapped. That kept us cooler.

Nadzab was an immense city of war. American strength had grown so that squadron after squadron of fighters and bombers were scattered among its many steel-mat runways. A hospital was set up to take care of the Australian infantrymen who got hurt up in the hills to the north, where we could hear the twenty-five-pounder field guns hammering away in the distance. There was a rest camp for the Australian Ninth Division. We were wryly amused that what we considered the front lines (my God, we could hear the guns, couldn't we?) the Australians considered a rest and rehabilitation center.

There was also a POW compound. It was an open corral of hurricane fencing, ten feet high, with two Australian MPs, each about seven feet high, watching it. Inside were two men. One was a thin, wretchedly malarial youth who grinned aimlessly at the people that stood outside, staring in. He was a Korean, sup- posedly filled with hatred for the Japanese, and he by gesture cadged cigarettes and waited to die of his multiple illnesses. The other was a muscular, impassive man with short black hair who sat, silent and motionless in the center of the compound, as far from the sightseers as he could get. He was a Japanese. He ob- viously hated the Korean—and everyone else—and he stared at nothing for hours at a time and waited to die of his shame at having been taken alive. The MPs looked after them stolidly, keeping people away as much as possible, until the time came to ship them south to a permanent POW camp in Australia. It was said that not many prisoners ever got there because the MPs were fond of opening the doors of the C-47s, over the Arafura Sea, and kicking them out.

Nadzab had movies. They were held outside in a Corps of Engineers camp about a mile from our squadron, and we went every time the program changed. We were starved for them after Tsili-Tsili, where the only entertainment was those native dogs copulating.

We saw Mickey Rooney charm his little tiny way into the heart of Judy Garland over and over again. We saw Van Johnson shoot down evil Japanese pilots who flew AT-6s and hissed, "Die, you Yankee dog!" and bucked and writhed and spilled black blood from between their big teeth as Van clobbered them and then went home a hero to win his way into Priscilla Lane's heart with his true-blue freckle-faced Americanness. We saw Betty Grable dancing away on those incredible legs while Gene Kelly yearned for her and Phil Silvers said, "How *are* ya? Nice to *see* ya," to rich entrepreneur Vincent Price, and Kelly went off to fight the rotten, yellow Japs, and when he came back wounded, he saw her going out with Vincent Price and skulked in a dark alley outside the good old stage door, heartbroken and too proud to show himself, shattered as he was, until Donald O'Connor found him and spilled the beans that Grable was really mad for him, not Vincent; and so when she got to the final big number at the Palace, Gene sang the verse to their song from behind stage and then came on to dance his way into her heart even though both kneecaps had been shot off by the dirty Japs somewhere in the Pacific.

We all went faithfully, every time, like school kids going to a museum. And the thing I remember best is flicking a scorpion off the collar of Riznik's moldy trench coat while he sat very still just in front of me.

Aside from fun time, Gopher was given some scary things to do. No longer did we escort milk runs to Wau or similar out-posts, or play with our Boomerang friends in areas where enemy planes seldom ventured. Instead we had a number of strafing assignments, a bit more dive-bombing, and scramble after scramble to intercept what usually turned out to be thun-derstorms. One of these scrambles turned into the most danger-ous mission I ever flew.

We had finished a long day's work, flying patrols, and as the sun inched down, the cumulus buildup over the mountains boiled up to meet it until one creamy shoulder of cloud hunched in front of it. Instantly the shadow was flung across the great island, and the kunai lost its breathless heat. Sweat dried on our bare torsos and we walked out of the alert tent to look at the hills and feel a little of the delight of earth and sky and clouds and pleasant warmth and empty space.

Airedale kicked off his boots and shorts and went into the shower we had rigged from a 110-gallon belly tank, cleverly valved by a string. By the end of the day the water was quite hot. This was that time, and we were ready to move back to camp and have a drink.

We didn't even hear the phone ring because we expected no calls. But Badger appeared at the side of the tent and shouted, "Scramble! Four flights, angels twenty! Get 'em into the murk, boys. This looks like a real one!"

Gopher had a reputation of being a bunch of reasonably com-petent veterans, not very eager, not a stamping ground for aces, but able to fulfill, after a fashion, the most basic and imperative of its duties. This time the squadron was caught short. People started running for planes, then remembered that they didn't have their guns and started back to get them, then decided to hell with them, and turned back to the planes again. Airedale came out of the shower, glistening wet, wrapped a towel around his waist and was in his cockpit before anyone else. Riznik tried to run while zipping up his flying suit, tripped over a flapping leg, tore the thing off and jumped into his plane in shorts alone. Morgan, who had been playing catch with Steve and me, was already trying to snap up his parachute harness before he realized he still had a baseball glove on.

My personal reaction was one of outrage. I bargained for a ten-hour day of churning adrenalin, grinding bowels, cottony mouth and other symptoms of quivering cowardice. As far as I was concerned, the whistle had blown for today. But to avoid this particular overtime was going to take either inspiration, which was remarkably absent, or a sudden physical seizure, which would have appeared to the others unlikely since I had noisily been playing catch.

I had sublime faith in Nanette. She would think of something. Yet when I sprang into her cockpit, her knobs and levers and hinges all remained firmly in place; when I ground her up she came to life with great good humor—no groans and mucusy coughs. The first thing I knew, I was leading my flight off the strip in the gathering twilight, with Nanette purring like an affectionate ocelot. "What the hell is wrong with you?" I asked her. "You got a death wish?" But she paid no attention, simply climbing sweetly toward 20,000 feet.

Of course she knew what she was doing. As we were nearing 15,000 feet the sector called us home. There wasn't a Nip within 100 miles; the radar had tuned onto some imaginary target—a heavy rain cloud or a high flight of birds or maybe a flying saucer—and it was now, "Thank you, Gopher, that's all for today."

I was very glad, because it was cold at 15,000 feet. We were having a sunset up there, and the night air was sifting in through the cracks in the fuselage, and I pitied poor Airedale wrapped in his towel and Riznik in his short pants. Quickly, we began to spiral down and as we looked earthward we all winced.

The earth we had left in the touch of a setting sun was now swallowed by night. Though our own planes were gilded with the last rays, there was nothing below us to indicate land or sea, mountain or jungle. A dark, opaque curtain had been drawn while we were away.

Ah, well, we thought, there is always more light than we think. There is always the horizon to be found as pupils dilate. A bad thing cannot happen to *me*.

We continued our letdown, and the gilding faded from our wings, and then we were wrapped in dark grayness and our eyes adjusted gradually as we frantically kept track of each other.

"Let's get the wing-tip lights on," said Rabbit in my earphones.

Jesus Christ. Which switch? I had never flown Nanette with lights. I had never turned them on in *any* P-39. I fumbled around the dashboard with my left hand while still holding the spiral with my right. Certain things I could recognize by touch, but the area where the light switches were arrayed was unexplored territory. I hadn't flown at night since AT-6 days, and the switch setup was different.

Most of Gopher was as ill-trained as I, and soon the complaints came in on the headset:

"Does anybody know where the fucking switch is?"

"Don't get your landing light by mistake; you'll do a slow roll."

"Hey Rabbit, I almost blew up my radio."

I recalled that the landing light on a 39 swung down from one wing as it went on. If you weren't prepared to compensate, the light acted like an aileron and would indeed roll you. I also remembered that the ship had been fitted with a destruct switch for the radio so that if you crash-landed somewhere near the Japs, you could keep them from finding out what sort of marvelous American electronics you had on board. Since their radio equipment was said to be considerably better than ours, we had trouble explaining to ourselves the need for that particular switch.

"Use a match to find it," said Rabbit. "Keep spread out, Gopher. Gentle turns."

In my eagerness to prevent myself from being blown to a pulp by igniting cockpit fumes, I had long given up smoking in flight, and didn't carry matches any more. But my groping left hand closed at last around a small bulb with a metal hood part way around it. I seemed to remember a thing simply called "cockpit lamp." Right under it was a toggle switch in the down position.

"Well," I said to Nanette, "I don't know if this is your radio or what, but here goes." Bracing myself to fight off that sudden roll from the landing light, I snapped the switch.

The cockpit was suddenly bright as day, and in horror I knew that I was blinding myself for future purposes, since my eyes were rapidly readjusting. Trying not to look at that blazing bulb which would leave a purple print on my retinas long after I turned it off, I quickly scanned the switch panel. At last: "navigation lights." I snapped them on and snapped the cockpit light off. Sure enough, I was seeing purple in my head, but a glance out my left window showed me a fine red light, and to the right, green shone merrily.

Around me now, I could see other reds and greens and was able to avoid them. Formation seemed to be about lost as we circled gently toward the strip—or at least where we felt it should be. And as the altimeter unwound, I could feel the air warming and I shivered gratefully.

And then the worst thing that ever happened to me while flying happened: The armor glass fogged up.

A P-39 had a nicely streamlined, curved canopy, tastefully rounded in front. But since it was supposed to be a combat plane and have bits of metal fired at it with serious intentions, the army, with its overriding terror of all those moms back home, decided that the pilot should be protected from being shot in the face by a square slab of bulletproof glass that stood upright above the dashboard and met the windscreen at its corners. It provided a flat surface for the light image of the gunsight, but as protection it was a silly idea. Any hurtling metal that struck it would have already struck the propeller, producing a vibration that would eventually cripple the plane. The bullet would also destroy the canopy, without which the plane would be virtually unflyable (at least Nanette would have been, with me flying her). The armor might deflect a bullet from striking the pilot right in his dimples—so dear to Mom—but it wouldn't safeguard him from all the bullets that came through the nose section below the windscreen. I guess the theory was that he could still look like the cream of America's crop even though his guts were being torn to sausage meat.

The armor glass was uniquely American in another respect too: It was a marvelous piece of engineering. The slab was about an inch and a half thick, made of tempered glass, so perfectly clear that pilots simply forgot it was there. I never saw glass so absolutely clear before or since. The trouble was, there was no way to get a cloth between the plane's curved windscreen and the straight edge of the armor glass so you could clean the side away from you. You had to unscrew the thing.

The result of this situation was that I was totally blinded by fog on the armor glass that I couldn't get at to wipe off. Judging from the wails over the radio, so was everyone else. Blinded, in the dark, while traveling 165 miles an hour in a small, highly unstable aircraft toward a landing strip that could not be seen and that ran down a valley between 800-foot hills, equally invisible! It was enough to make me surrender to the first rotten little yellow-bellied, bucktoothed, nearsighted, bandy-legged, bloodlusting, nun-raping Japanese that happened along. "Take me!" I would have begged. "Put me on a death march. Set me to work on a jungle railroad. Give me a diet of weevily rice. Grind out your horrid Oriental cigarettes on my private parts. Just get me the hell out of this!"

By opening a window, I could catch glimpses of what lay ahead. The slipstream whirled into the cockpit, and I got my goggles down quickly to keep the dust out of my eyes. But the goggles were tinted, giving me a badly underexposed view of what was essentially darkness, anyway. I pushed them up on my helmet again and squinched my eyes almost shut, hoping the tornado of air would blow the dust out of the cockpit.

What instruments remained in Nanette (most were removed from these planes to cut down on weight) indicated a normal rate of descent at normal speed. I could make out enough horizon visually to feel I was gently unwinding. No sweat. Only trouble was: no strip, either.

I cannot remember the rate of my heartbeat, the pressure of my pulse, the gasping speed of respiration. I do remember a sense of greater effort than I have ever experienced. My mind was racing, my touch on the controls was light and sure, but as quick as a blink. I was endlessly repeating a sharp, explosive vulgarity as I fought with all my soul for life. I have sometimes wondered since if other doomed people, Custer, maybe, went to their deaths murmuring "Shit, shit, shit, shit, shit . . ." Lee, dying at Lexington, Virginia, said, "Strike the tent." Jackson, succumbing to a light wound and a heavy death wish after Chancellorsville, said, "Let us cross over the river and rest in the shade of the trees." Washington, stricken by pneumonia and weariness, said, "It is well." But all these died in bed. Take Armistead at Gettysburg, leading the final remnant of Pickett's charge and seeing the Yankee rifles leveled at him. He might have said, "Shit." Davy Crockett at the Alamo, helplessly watching the gates crash open and the Mexicans come at him with leveled bayonets, may have found it a handy expression. The expletive seems a natural choice for Custer on his bare hillside along the Little Bighorn. And it certainly sprang readily and unwittingly to my lips as I descended toward flaming death in the New Guinea darkness.

My plane continued to sink happily toward destruction. No shying away, no nervous twitching, no complaint of any kind. For a moment I wondered if this was really Nanette. Had I somehow, in the rush of the scramble, taken the wrong aircraft? But it had been John who trussed me up in the cockpit, and with my left hand I could feel electrician's tape around the throttle knob where the Bakelite had cracked. Nanette, all right.

We were down to 1,000 feet, turning gently toward looming black hulks that I could see out the left window. The darkness was almost complete. The armor plate was completely fogged where I couldn't reach it. The radio was silent. I could see navigational lights far ahead of me, but they told me nothing. I was simply going to plow in, along with a lot of other guys, and the best hope was that maybe some engineer would read the intelligence reports on the catastrophe and work out a way to keep armor glass from fogging up.

With the dry sickness of a lover scorned, I now contemplated the fact that my dear, devilish, cowardly, playful little creature was nothing, except in my mind. She was not Nanette. She was a plane, an "it," a lousy, useless, war-losing P-39, dumbly doing what I, and I alone, made it do. My life-giving obsession of the last many months was mere fantasy. A plane is a plane is a plane. Shit, shit, shit.

The red and green lights ahead of me now rose and moved off to the left. From my left window, straining against the buffeting slipstream, I could sense that we were sinking between the looming black ridges. I wrenched my head inside and glared at the altimeter: 600 feet. The end was coming very quickly, and I had a feeling of no control over it, over anything. I wasn't flying this strange and futile aircraft, this "it." I was just sitting here, waiting, all alone. And it kept right on blithely lowering itself into the pit, insensible of the imminent end when it would dash itself—and me—against a warm hillside and light the night with its flames.

Head out the window again. Instinct for survival very strong. My brain had given up, but the instinct made me fly around in my harness—head out, head in, hands moving restlessly, but with no effect on the plane. Fight! Fight! Fight! The voice of a football coach from distant youth berating eleven muddy, scrawny teen-age players: "A team that won't be beaten, can't be beaten!" Oh, yeah?

My God, lights! A path of lights just ahead. Stretching away to hide behind the fogged glass. A runway, for Christ's sake!

Chop throttle. Landing light on and compensate. Flaps and wheels. Hold off. Get speed off. Can't see a fucking thing.

Squeak. Rattle. On the ground with a landing that wouldn't break an egg. Taxi straight. Call on radio: "Gopher, from Nanette. I'm on the strip safely. Landing light still on." And a series of voices. "Got you Nanette," "Thanks, buddy." "Right behind you."

A few minutes later we were all in the dimly lit alert tent. All of us. All sixteen. We were strangely quiet, for once, just staring at each other and smiling rather gently in the warmth of our fraternity. I snubbed out my cigarette and walked out and down to the dark revetment, where John was tying her down with help from a flashlight. I smiled at him, and he said, "I got a ride back on the crew chiefs' jeep. Want a lift?"

"Yes, I said. "I just want to see her, first."

I ran my hand around her nose section and touched the tar stain.

"Honey," I said. "You're really something."

Then I got in beside John and rode up to camp.

Nanette was treated with a sort of awe by the rest of the squadron after that night scramble. My relationship with her was fully recognized and largely envied, though Rabbit grumbled that it was setting an awkward precedent to allow a pilot to carry on like this with an airplane. "What would the people back home think?" he demanded one evening when the whiskey ration had just arrived and we were getting through it as quickly as possible.

"Screw them," said Badger, who was listening. "I'm more worried about Park. He's got himself hooked up with a real bitch, and he's such a dumb-ass she'll probably kill him."

"You don't know her, Badger," I said.

"I flew the whore once," he answered. "That was enough."

"She certainly tried to kill *me*," Rabbit put in. "I kid you not. We should have broken her up right then."

"If you had, you'd still be orbiting the area waiting for your armor glass to unfog," I protested, hotly.

Rabbit mumbled something and refilled my canteen cup. "We're getting some replacements in," he said. "And I don't want their little heads all filled with this kind of shit. You got that, Park?"

"I won't say a thing," I answered. "Let them go have an affair with their own planes."

The conversation arose because we had begun flying occasional patrols far northward, well into Nip country, and Nanette was neatly sidestepping each one that turned out to be the least bit perilous. One day when I went out to mount her, prepared to die for Old Glory and the Christian ethic, I found John staring sorrowfully at a flat tire.

"Son of a bitch was fine when I preflighted her," he said. "Just went down a few minutes ago. Must be a hairy mission this morning, Lieutenant."

"That's my girl," I said, and walked happily back to the alert tent to watch fifteen planes take off and then to write some letters. In three hours they came over, whistling from their untaped gun muzzles, belly tanks gone. I counted fourteen planes and watched one do a victory roll over the strip. Carter had become an ace, and Riznik was missing, and I felt sick.

Then for two missions of the same sort, Nanette was fine. We saw nothing, and all my adrenalin served no purpose. But the next time, just as we were forming up after takeoff, my door popped open and it was impossible to close it in flight. I tried everything—opening windows and slamming it, shutting it with steady pressure—nothing worked. The door was held ajar by whirling slipstream, and with her flight attitude affected, Nanette flew exactly like a crab—partly sideways. She had no hope of keeping up with the others so I called in a shame-faced "snafu" and turned back, a lamed bitch heading for the kennels while the rest of the pack, lean and purposeful, streaked off on a warm scent.

Again, they found the fox. I returned, taxied up to John, muttered something to him, slammed the door a couple of times (of course it worked perfectly on the ground) and went back to the alert tent to play solitaire and listen to fighter frequency on the radio. And within five minutes I heard those voices, high-pitched with excitement, calling out those familiar phrases that sent the pulse racing:

"Gopher leader, bandits eleven o'clock high. . . ."

"I've got them. Switch tanks and drop, Gopher."

"Blue Two, close up on me."

"Four Tonies at nine!"

It sounds so drearily old-fashioned now—a John Wayne movie at half after midnight. But even I, with all of Nanette's protective ploys, heard it often enough back then so that I still sometimes wake with a sweaty start in the silence of the night, the voices echoing in my ears from an uneasy dream.

They came less frequently after that overture. The radio hummed with tension, then suddenly erupted with semicoherent words: ". . . On your tail, Morgan!" Eight seconds of hum. ". . . Left! left! left!" Fifteen seconds of hum. ". . . Shit!" Twelve seconds of hum. "Can you make it home OK?" "I think so, but hang around, will you?" "You bet your ass." Silence—silence—silence.

I gave them forty minutes and then went outside to wait for them. It was a lonely forty minutes, a time of much thinking, and when I stepped out from the tent and felt the physical blow of the heat I had reached the conclusion that Nanette was getting to be an embarrassment. Her care for me was unfair to the others. Why should I be shielded from combat, and no one else? They all deserved it as much as I. They were nearly all equally afraid—except for Badger, who obviously wanted to die in the cockpit, and Carter, who was a fool.

A distant howling, whistling snarl reached my ears. Looking northward I saw them coming in low: a flight of four, another flight of four, a flight of three (oh, my God), an element of two, and then, very low and heading straight in, wheels down, another element of two. With a surge of relief I realized that the flight of three was my own—I was the missing plane. They were all home. But there was something quite wrong with that last element, now slowing, flaps down, noses high, as if they were going to land in formation—which was a pretty tricky thing to do on those strips.

The leader did land, rolled to the end of the metal, pulled off and then just sat there, propeller idly turning; door still closed. The wingman jammed on his throttle, tucked up his wheels and staggered up and around the traffic pattern, cutting it very close and coming in quickly. He taxied up beside the leader's plane, halted and chopped off his engine. I saw the door open and a figure climb out on the wing, jump down and then run over to the idling plane. By then I was running, too, for I knew whoever was inside was hurt.

It was Piss-Ant. I recognized his squadron number. Steve stood on the wing beside him, half-hidden as he reached inside the cockpit to shut off the engine. I was beside the wing myself, panting, and the other planes were landing around us, and pale, smudged faces were turning anxiously toward us from the open windows as they taxied past.

"Help me with him," Steve said.

I climbed up beside him, aware that something was wrong with Piss-Ant's plane. Of course: the canopy was askew, the way mine had been that time, long ago, when I accidentally snap-rolled on top of a loop. But there was a better reason for this situation: a twisted and fractured strip of metal that had once been one of the crosspieces . . . a large hole plunging through the Plexiglas with cracks radiating from it . . . a second hole a foot away . . . something dark smearing the inside of the broken canopy—dark and, oh, sweet Jesus, bright red.

Piss-Ant was unconscious, slumped to one side. He looked all right. Steve and I got the last straps and clips undone and eased him out on the wing. And then I felt the wet on my hands. A jeep skidded to a halt beside us, and we were able to get him on the hood and hold him while we jounced back to the alert tent.

A 20-millimeter cannon shell had exploded in the cockpit beside Piss-Ant. His body was like a wet sponge—a mass of little holes seeping blood. Sitting beside him on the hood of the jeep, holding him, I felt it dampen the frayed fabric of my khaki shorts.

"Those Tonies are bastards," Steve said, holding Piss-Ant's shoulders. "Little and sharp-nosed and fast. They're scary."

We got the medics, and Piss-Ant was taken away to base hospital and in two weeks stopped in to see us, strangely pale beside all our yellow-brown faces; and he was pretty slow and feeble in his movements, but the same old Piss-Ant. He suddenly came into the alert tent and there was a roar of voices all talking at once, and people reached toward him as though to pound him on the back, then thought better of it. We were delighted with Piss-Ant and with ourselves and with life itself.

"What happened, Piss-Ant? You forget to cross yourself?"

"Damn sloppy landing, Piss-Ant. Watch it."

"How's the hospital? Didja get any?"

And Piss-Ant grinned and grinned, and then sat down on a cot and grinned. And he said he was by God going home—how about *that?*—and that he couldn't remember landing at all, but he remembered being annoyed by Steve's voice in his earphones telling him to get the nose up and chop the throttle and touch left rudder and a whole lot more stuff that seemed like such a lot of useless hard work. He looked at Steve: "I kept wanting to tell you not to be such a horse's ass."

Then it was time for Piss-Ant to go, and he got up sort of carefully and looked at us all and touched Steve on the arm and then walked off with Rabbit, and we heard the jeep drive off.

It was that evening that Rabbit and Badger and I were killing off the whiskey ration and talking about Nanette.

"How long does that Goddamn bitch think she can go on ducking missions?" Badger asked, staring into his cup.

"I can't read her mind," I said. "But she's pretty determined."

"It just isn't right," said Rabbit. "She's starting to run the squadron. That's what she's starting to do, by God."

"Kick her ass out," said Badger, draining his cup. "Send her down to some training squadron in Australia."

I shook my head. "She'd just kill someone within a week."

Rabbit suddenly looked up, inspired. "We might let the Japs capture her," he said. "Then she could kill one of them."

"If you're going to talk like that, you can give me back my bottle," I said.

"Are we onto your bottle?" Badger asked. He topped off the cups.

The upshot of the evening was that Badger got drunk. He always built a high floor for his tent—he was a good carpenter—and when he was drunk, which was every night, and needed to relieve himself, he would roll to the edge of his cot, which was right at the edge of his flooring, and then let go over the side without having to get up. This night he was drunk enough so he got confused and rolled to the wrong side, and let go into one of his Australian flying boots. That made him very angry all next day.

Another upshot was that Rabbit wrote a letter to Piss-Ant's wife, who, he said, had just married him for the allotment checks. He wrote it very fast: "Listen, you two-bit whore, Piss-Ant is being sent to a stateside hospital because he got clobbered by a Tony, which is an airplane about 700 times better than the shit they give us to fly. He's got 16,000 little holes in him, and he's going to seep through them for a while, but then he'll be OK. But it's the end of the gravy train for you. So either get out or start loving him."

He sent it off through channels, and of course it came back right away from Group with a little note from the group commander: "Come on, Rabbit. Get your finger out of your ass and write the 'Next-of-Kin, Wounded in Action' letter which you'll find in the brown book." So he wrote a letter full of phrases like "deep regrets," and "I know that you will share our pride," and "during which he conducted himself with the utmost gallantry." It slid right through channels.

The final upshot was that I got assigned, two days later, to Number 70, Badger's plane (he was still too hung over to fly) as Red Flight leader on a mission into Tony country. I drove to Number 70's revetment that morning by a route that would not take me past Nanette. Hell, do you swing past your mistress's apartment when you're on your way to meet a call girl at the corner bar? I grunted at 70's crew chief and he snarled at me, and away I went on my little adventure.

She did it very well. She was really awfully good at it, and it was exciting. But I was tense and a little unsure of myself all through the flight up there. And then the bad part happened. We spotted Tonies way above us, and they all flashed in the early sun as they rolled on their backs. And then they were howling down on us in a split S, so happy to see us again and be able to play with us some more.

I was too blind with terror to remember much about the soiree. They swarmed all over my flight and Yellow Flight, but we had kept Blue and White Flights a fair way back of us. So when the Tonies came in on us, Blue and White were able to come in on them with one good pass. No one got any, but for a few seconds the sky was all filled with Tonies climbing the hell out of there, standing on their tails, and 39s diving the hell out of there, standing on their noses. That ended the party—except for one Goddamn late-stayer who'd been sucking hot saki for breakfast and must have recognized Number 70 as belonging to a fellow drunk. Anyway, he came at me, head on—a little flat line that grew into an airplane in the blink of an eye because we were meeting each other at about 700 miles an hour. I had an impression of flickering light along his wings, and although I have no memory of firing back, I felt the fumes in my eyes so I guess I was. Then I knew he was going to ram me, and I banged the stick forward, and everything turned red as the blood surged up into my eyeballs.

The next thing I knew he was gone, and at the same instant there was a bang on my right wing, and I looked out and saw a big gaping hole in the leading edge. I eased out of my dive, very gingerly, and the wing stayed on OK, so we gathered together, a little shakily, and flew on home.

Number 70 now tended to swerve to the right, and if I let her slow down, her right wing would want to drop, but she was really no trouble to fly home. I didn't buzz the strip, however. I just brought her in. And of course there was Badger following me in a jeep as soon as I landed. He trailed me into his revetment and jumped on the wing as I closed her down.

"Jesus Christ," he said. "Now what?"

"A little trouble with the right wing," I said. "She flew quite nicely, though. She seems like a nice plane. I'm glad you let me try her."

"Oh, shut up," he said, jumping down again to stare into the hole in the wing.

The crew chief joined Badger, and as I climbed out, one of them reached deep inside the hole and retrieved something shiny. They passed it back and forth and then handed it to me. An ejected 20-millimeter cannon shell with Japanese markings on it. I had almost managed to be the only brave, skillful, glamorous fly-boy in the history of the United States to be shot down by an ejected shell.

Next day I was reassigned to Nanette, and, in a desperation move by Rabbit and Badger, was made squadron leader for a barge hunt. It was a jujitsu stunt—suddenly adding your own weight to your opponent's thrust and so overpowering and destroying him. Everyone knew Nanette liked low-level work. OK, the bitch would get it, leading the Goddamn squadron.

I had been squadron leader before, when all the good pilots were stricken with a recurrence of dysentery, and I had been on barge hunts before and loved them. You stayed very low and very fast, sizzling just over the water along a stretch of the north coast. You kept close to shore, peeking under the drooping palm fronds where the enemy were apt to moor their supply barges. If you saw anything suspicious, even a pile of brush that might be camouflage piled over a barge, you whanged away.

Two flights did this nice duty, and the other two stooged around at about three or four thousand feet, keeping an eye

peeled for those damn Tonies. I think Rabbit and Badger were
honestly hoping we'd get bounced by the Tonies, or failing that,
would poke our noses into a clump of ack-ack that had been
practicing on sea gulls, as we were convinced the Japs did—
they were awfully good—and that Nanette would get shot out of
the sky and all Gopher's troubles would be over. I think Rabbit
and Badger had not given much thought to the strong probabil-
ity that old Park would get blasted into a red haze along with
Nanette. I'm sure they wished me no personal ill. They just
didn't think about it.

I thought about it. I woke abruptly in the middle of the night
and stared at the faint, cloudy shroud of my mosquito bar, and
through it at the dark inside of the tent, and out the open fly at
the sky made luminous by a bombers' moon, and I thought with
a sudden, wrenching panic that I, by God, did not the least want
to die. I had often had these thoughts, suddenly waking me with
twists of fear. When I was a new pilot I prayed and I went to
chaplain's services sometimes, but the group padre was more
concerned with telling people that it was wrong to swear and
drink and screw than with reassuring them that the chances were
pretty good that they *would* live, and that if they *did* buy it,
there was something else besides life . . . I don't know. Something.

I never heard a padre who could talk to a frightened pilot.

In the squadron we supported each other by analyzing mistakes and finding reasons for death. We rationalized that if we
could avoid the reasons we could avoid dying. Swearing and
drinking and screwing helped a great deal, too. But when the
doubts came on you in the middle of the night, you felt lonely.

I stared out at the moonlight and thought, Golly, I wonder if
tomorrow's the big day for me. Or will I be lying in this sack
tomorrow night, grateful that I've gotten through another

day—as I am now—and wondering about the day after tomorrow? And how many days after that, God? How long does it go on?

Then I thought, Well, anyway, I'm back with Nanette. She'll think of something. And the tension drained quietly away and I went back to sleep.

We took off early, Nanette tucking up her wheels and biting into the virginal air, for there was no plane in front of us. A gentle turn to the right, and my wingman, a new guy named Faversham, seemed shaky as he tried to hold position. He seemed to want to slide under me and keep on the outside of the turn, but I made him stay, pointing a finger at my right wing. It suddenly occurred to me that this was what Badger had done to me, so long ago, only worse. Well, well.

Unlike Badger, I eased my turn so that the other flights could slide together neatly. Badger had always proselytized, always tried to convert the average flying school product into an old pro. I would not be a missionary.

At the end of a complete circle, all four flights were in the air and in position, noses up in a climb, wings banked to finish the turn—a pretty sight. I rolled gently to the level and steepened the climb. The air was like glass, and the fifteen other planes hung with me and behind me, motionless, it seemed; it was only the dark mountains that were moving.

I turned slightly toward those exaggerated shapes—the jagged tors and deeply undercut cliffs, never softened by the grinding of a glacier—and we slid through our usual pass, a landmark as familiar to us as the corner drugstore on Main Street. Our navigation was so visual in those days that we seldom bothered with compass courses except when we stooged off to intercept something. Our briefing before a mission did not tell us to fly 33 degrees for exactly forty-seven minutes and then change course to 342 degrees while descending to minimum altitude. "Go through the pass, then swing up the coast, keeping down on the deck," was what we understood.

So that's what we did. For a few minutes we could look down a little nervously on those dark valleys, still steaming from the night air, and look out at the impossibly steep slopes with their matting of towering trees, and wince at the sudden outcroppings of tumbled boulders, spilled languidly among the peaks by some primordial fury. And then the mountains dropped away and the sea gleamed before us, smooth and welcoming.

Nanette lowered her nose, and her speed picked up from a whisper to a hiss to a rush. At 5,000 feet I squeezed my mike button. "Gopher Blue and Yellow, hold it here. Red and White, let's go." And I steepened the dive, heading toward the sparkling waves.

We crossed the coast nearly perpendicular to it and going like hell, so that any coastal batteries would have less chance to tune in on us. Nanette and I were nothing if not careful about matters like that. Then, down close to the waves, I brought the two low flights into a wide turn that sent us angling back to the coast with the sun behind us. We could see beautifully; the Nips would have a hard time picking us up against the low morning sun. I was very proud of myself for all this.

This was a lovely stretch of New Guinea. The land was high until it reached the water and it was all kunai grass. It looked like green rangeland from the air, except that the eight- or ten-foot-tall grass waved and rippled with every puff of air, giving it a silky, almost liquid quality. This high ground ended abruptly in steep cliffs which tumbled to a strip of beach. The cliffs were not solid rock, so wave action from storms had undercut them in places, and runoffs from the high ground had cut deep gullies in them and scoured pools in their bases. Here was where the barges were supposed to be hiding, shielded by the tall palms that grew where cliffs met sand. I was struck again, as I had been on my first missions out of Moresby, by the luck of the enemy. The Japanese still had a firm grip on all the beauty of the island. The Allies had been left with the flat, swampy southern coast with its dense rain forest, its bugs and snakes and scorpions and scrofulous natives. But after all, we had Coca Cola. That's more than they could say.

A voice: "Gopher leader from Gopher Blue, there's a Zeke in the kunai on top of the next point."

"Roger," I answered, "we'll have a look."

I climbed to clear the cliff top, and there, nestled in the grass, plain as day, was an abandoned Japanese fighter. It must have force-landed—perhaps after a run-in with those courageous killers from Gopher Squadron—and been left because it was impossible to remove. It was painted a splotchy pink and yellow, the camouflage for a coral airstrip. That meant it came from some base farther along the coast. There wasn't much coral here. The red circles stood out starkly against the faded paint, giving me that jolt that I always felt when I saw them—My God! There they are! Right there!—even though the plane now marked only a harmless memory. The canopy was open, and I pictured the Nip pilot climbing out of it disgustedly, reaching in again to retrieve his maps and maybe blow up his radio, considering whether to close his canopy against the ravaging weather and then saying the hell with it and walking off.

"Gopher leader, let's clobber it."

"No," I snapped. "Forget it."

"Roger."

A curious exchange. Whoever it was wanted to see an undamaged Japanese plane in his sights and blow it to pieces.

Why not? But I had reacted from the gut without any thought at all. Why? I could hear now the mild complaint when we returned: someone saying, "Hey, we saw a ditched Zeke on top of a cliff—just sitting there in the kunai without a mark on her. Park wouldn't let us blow her up. Shee-it." What would I say? Let's see: "The gunfire would have warned everyone that we were coming." Or, "It would have been a waste of ammo—we hadn't even seen a barge yet." Or, "Nanette wouldn't let me." Or simply, "She was harmless, so who cares?" Anyway, we flicked over her and left her to become a perfectly preserved memorial to all that strange, old-fashioned time. I know someone must have found her and either destroyed her out of the frustration of defeat, or cannibalized her to salvage something from the wreckage of hopes, or turned her into a god and worshipped her, or casually blown her up in the offhand savagery of the newly triumphant, or perhaps joyfully eased her onto a coastal lighter and shipped her to a museum. But I hope she's on that cliff, faded to her bare aluminum, beaten down by decades of tropical storms, yet still a monument of sorts.

A long beach curved gently away from the point, and we spun along it, just over the mild surf. It was buff-colored sand, alluvial, not coral, a little darker than, say, Coney Island. Coney Island without people, with only eight drab little fighter planes skittering barely above it, searching for certain small things to destroy—Dodgem cars, perhaps, or maybe cotton candy machines.

I spotted a small gap in the beach leading into a dark, palm-shaded pocket of backwater. That was exactly where the Dodgems would be hidden. I was past it before I could turn, but I called it in quickly: "Gopher White, I'm just passing an inlet."

White Flight instantly wheeled out to sea, then curved back in at the inlet, firing as they came. I was too busy flying six feet off the deck to pay much attention, but they said nothing, so probably they hit nothing of any importance. The action dropped them astern of Red Flight. Then I saw a brush pile on the beach ahead of me, and got in a short burst before flicking over it. My second element made a weaving turn, out and in, to get a longer shot at it.

Thus we strung ourselves out as we searched: Nanette humming peacefully in the still air, Faithful Faversham glued close beside and behind, his eyes far too much on me instead of the world around him—the standard mistake of all new pilots—then my second element, Morgan and another new guy chasing after him, then Carter leading White Flight, which by now was all in line astern.

We clung to the shoreline, rounding the points, peering into the coves, peeking under the trees. And suddenly, at the end of one point, there was a round, man-made structure, an earthwork with something protruding outward from it—my God, a gun emplacement!

Everyone saw it, of course, and I knew all eyes were on Nanette to see how she would react. So I swung out to give myself a second more time, then turned on the cannon switch and laid the sight on the target. "Now, baby," I pleaded with her, "for Christ's sake show what you can do," and I touched the trigger.

Whump-whump. That was all she needed. The first shell hit the lip of the emplacement, sending up a spurt of dirt; the second landed smack inside, and odd objects erupted.

"Beautiful!" said Carter's voice, and I decided to like him.

"Sweetheart," I murmured to Nanette, "I didn't know you were a killer all this time," and then we were over the target and we banked vertically to look down into it.

Logs of wood, carefully cut to resemble guns, were scattered about by the exploding shell. That was all. Nanette had, typically, wiped out a fake gun emplacement, set up by the Japanese to draw fire from suckers, maybe just for laughs.

Nanette was nothing if not firm in her purpose. If that had been a real emplacement, she would have missed it, or her cannon would have failed to fire, or her engine would have quit just as I got the sight lined up, or one wheel would have suddenly come down, or *something*. Since it was a phony, and since I had asked her to behave, she had delighted in showing the whole squadron what she could do. Why did I ever have these doubts about her, anyway? I burst out laughing into my oxygen mask, and then, since clock and fuel gauge dictated it, we swung around for the return run.

Now we had a different visual angle and we found a few more targets along the shore and happily shot off our guns at piles of palm fronds, dark niches behind the beach, one outrigger canoe that we'd already strafed on the way up, a palm tree with a platform (empty) built around it, and a rounded heap of sand. Having thus furthered the march toward victory over the

forces of evil, we simply flew quietly just above the twinkling sea for a little while, working back into formation, the top flights parading with us, 5,000 feet overhead.

It was one of them that called in two boats headed up the coast toward us, coming fast, according to the wakes. "PTs, probably," said the voice.

In a moment I saw two specks on the horizon. They grew fast, sprouting high white bow waves. I was almost certain that they were PT boats, but there was always the need to check out everything, so we held course toward them a little longer.

"They're ours," snapped Blue Flight, overhead. "White star on the deck."

I climbed and turned sharply away so that our eight planes also showed their stars. Then we turned back and settled down to pass them, Nanette waggling her wings as an added precaution against getting shot down by the U.S. Navy. And thus we flashed by one another—eight P-39s in drab green or splotchy camouflage, all with yellow noses, the leader wearing a black smear of tar, and two PT boats in navy dark blue with white numbers on them, smashing through the waves. I lifted my hand in greeting, inside my canopy, and aboard the nearest boat a couple of men wearing khaki shorts and nice tans waved back. Beside them a third man was crouched behind a long-barreled machine gun, tracking me in his sight, just for practice.

We were now ready for the pass and home. I brought the two low flights upstairs while the two top flights wove back and forth to stay in position with us until we were all together. Then all sixteen planes settled into a long, boring climb toward the mountains. I loosened my Sutton harness and managed to pry my cramped buttocks off the seat to let blood flow through them. We sat on rubber dinghies, intricately folded on top of our parachute packs. An undoubtedly apocryphal story circulated among us that a P-39 pilot, crammed into his tiny cockpit, had inadvertently pulled the string that triggered the inflation cartridge of his dinghy. He was, according to the legend, almost crushed by the yellow monster that was suddenly born beneath him, snapping and writhing and growing obscenely, mashing him nearly helpless against the already confining roof of his canopy until at last he could free his sheath knife and stab the beast to hissing death. Anyway, the folded dinghies got very hard after you sat on them for three hours.

We were still climbing when we went through the pass, for clouds had started their tropical buildup on the other side of the range. The great boiling humps of cumulus rose so fast that even when we judged ourselves safely above them and leveled off to go over them, they managed to beat us to the rendezvous. We swerved to dash between them, barely eluding their vaporous grip, and then, free at last, we dropped our noses and howled down the other side of the obstruction, rolling and chandelling and snaking past the new crops of cloud that were beginning their growth.

We fell into line astern for this rat race, and Nanette led the sixteen in steep S-turns so that she was aimed for a moment straight at the Number Four man of Yellow Flight—Tail-Ass Charlie—before she swung to the next turn. She and I led this whip-cracking, I by simply leaning my body—willing her to do this, do that.

At last we were at our call-in point, and I called sector and identified us. Now we had to get rid of 8,000 feet of air so we could meet the ground again at Nadzab, so Nanette lay over on her side and began the tight spiral that would bring us all down.

I leaned to the left, and Nanette banked smoothly to the vertical. Now to tighten the turn: finger pressure on the stick, and her nose swung hard. More pressure, and condensation began to stream from the wing tips. I felt the centrifugal force build up, driving my chin toward my chest, my lower lids toward my cheeks. I held my breath and clamped my stomach muscles to send blood into my head and so clear my vision. At the same time, I raised a leaden left hand from the throttle quadrant to my nose, closed the nostrils, then blew to snap pressure back into my ears, for we were dropping rapidly.

At this point in a spiral, a P-39 would sometimes snap-roll and fall out of the turn. This was the typical "high-speed stall" that these little beasts were so fond of pulling on unwary pilots. But my fifteen followers were adequate-to-excellent P-39 drivers, and as I wrenched my head around I found them all with me, trailing around behind and above to form a corkscrew of airplanes.

Gently, with one finger only, I added back pressure on the stick, and Nanette responded smoothly, tightening her turn even more, until the contrails from the wing tips grew thick and creamy, etching the air behind me. Now I knew I was too tight for the others to follow, but I didn't care—this was a unique moment between lovers. I tightened again, just the faintest pressure, and now I felt the tiniest beginnings of a tremble under me. I was breathtakingly close to a snap, a stall, a tumble that would drop me uncontrollably into the jungle. "Augering in," we called it. "What happened to old Park," I could hear the voices saying. "Oh the poor bastard augered in one day and bought the farm."

Once more, insanely, I increased the pressure with one finger, and the tremble increased—still so faint that a new pilot would barely feel it, but a shout of alarm to me. And at last, as though waking from a dream, I relaxed my finger and felt the motion smooth out. Then, clearing my ears again, I checked the altimeter and saw that we were down where we should be. I rolled out of the turn, leaning my body back to the right and watched the horizon pivot around my nose and settle into place.

"Wow," said a voice, "that was really tearing the ass out of it."

Yes, I thought. And never again. Ever. For I had, momentarily, become part of Nanette—one and indivisible—and the two of us, in our ecstasy, had come very close to dying.

No plane is a person; no person a plane. No person is anything but a person—a single entity, in charge of his own mind and body and to some extent his destiny. But there are times when the interplay between two is so intense and absorbing that they do indeed seem fused into one. And I think one of the two can be a machine.

I knew, flying onto the strip that marvelous day, that I had touched something strange and secret. And I also knew that somehow it all had to end now for us. I was—we were—exploring something incredibly dangerous.

XIV

The End of It

On the day after that splendid—and shattering—mission, Nanette and I were given a rest. On the next day, eighteen Japanese Betty bombers came high over Nadzab and dropped their load of antipersonnel "daisy cutters" with devastating accuracy.

We were not in the air. Gopher had been kept on ground alert against the possibility of an enemy raid, which had been foretold by the coast watchers. Yet we had no Yellow alert. We had

only a Red—three fast shots by a great 90-millimeter antiaircraft
gun in a Connecticut National Guard battery a mile away.
Wham, wham, wham. And then, faintly, the undulating, fast-
fading sound of the shells climbing, and finally the three tiny
explosions, four miles high. If you hold your breath and let your
lips pop open three times, you have an idea of how they
sounded: *pa, pa, pa.*

We did not need to be told to get into the slit trenches. But on
the way, Steve and I paused to gaze up, almost in admiration, at
the glinting silver dots, high in the sky, moving over us in a
picture-postcard formation. The bombers formed Vs of three
planes each, which were compounded into a big V of nine
planes—we called it a V of Vs—and then this was repeated in a
second wave. They looked as though they were in an air show
for Flag Day. They also were right straight over us. There was
no doubt about it. If ever there was a case of planes being *directly* overhead it was that one. We looked, and we knew that
the bombs were already on the way, and we jumped into the
trench and cowered, waiting for them.

We heard them within a couple of seconds. They whisper as
they come down—wheeoh-*wheeoh*-WHEEOH-*WHEEOH!*—and
if they are heading right at you, the whisper becomes a rushing
clatter like a small train coming at you, insanely fast.

They began hitting a couple of hundred feet away, and they
walked inexorably toward us across the kunai, the whumping
explosions growing louder until they simply became great gongs
being struck inside our heads. The ground trembled, then
jumped in a sort of agony as the bombs struck closer and closer.
I dragged myself into the earth with my fingers. I thought of
nothing.

Blessedly, the explosions moved past us, grew fainter, stopped.
The air was filled with buzzes and smacks and plops as the

shrapnel whizzed and struck the earth and sizzled with heat. Very cautiously, we raised our heads and looked out into an opaque world of yellow-brown dust that reeked of cordite.

As the smoke and dust slowly blew away we crawled out, trembling, and walked toward a thick black column of smoke fed by savage flames in one of our revetments.

Nanette's revetment.

She had received a direct hit. It took her half an hour to burn. When the fire was finally out, there was nothing left of her except a small pile of fine white ash and a perfectly round metal disk, four inches in diameter and an inch thick, nicely machined, lying in the exact center of the ash pile. Gingerly, I picked it up, but it was quite cool. I still have it somewhere. I have no idea what it is. I used to tell friends that I thought it came from the planet Krypton, along with Superman, and the friends would smile.

Two other planes had been damaged; the alert tent was shredded by shrapnel; six pilots discovered that they had been nicked; and one crew chief had become a soggy red bundle of clothes at the bottom of a bomb-scorched slit trench. It was the crew chief for Number 75—the same man who had helped me get out of it when it had been shot up in that big raid on Moresby, all those months ago. He had been blown to bits.

I was given a new model P-39 and it was fine. In less than a month, Gopher Squadron was given P-47s and learned how to fly them. They were all right. They were big and heavy and honest and stupid. They did everything you asked them, blindly. We got pretty good with them, and then Charles Lindbergh came out and showed us how to fly extra-long-range missions in them. Seven hours of ass-cramp.

Operations got harder. There were no more barge hunts. New

people arrived and old people were sent home. Rabbit left, and we all got drunk, and Steve threw up. Steve was made commanding officer. Badger was ordered home, too, and he protested. He said he wanted to stay with the squadron and that if he was forced to go home he would make life miserable for everyone in Washington until they reassigned him back to Gopher. He was sent home anyway, and I was made operations officer in his place.

Steve was sent to Group headquarters on temporary duty, and I became acting CO of the squadron. I was never much of a pilot, but I did manage to shoot down a Tony in a P-47. After a while I was sent home, and we all got drunk, and Steve came over from Group and threw up.

Gopher Squadron eventually was given P-51s, and according to the people I knew who were still there at that time, this plane was so heart-wrenchingly beautiful that it almost came alive. But the war was very demanding by then. We were trying to win it, dashing up through the Philippines and all that, shooting down Nips right and left, taking losses. No one had any time to fall in love with a P-51.

Badger showed up. Apparently he had spread so much misery through the halls of the new Pentagon that he got himself reassigned to Gopher. On a mission in the Philippines he was hit and landed his 51 on a Japanese strip. When the Nips started coming out to get him, the rest of Gopher made a low pass over him and saw him slumped in the cockpit. And suddenly, with the enemy closing in on him to capture him and play with him until he died, the Gopher pilots began strafing him and they blew him up.

"It was the only thing we could do for him," Morgan told me, years later. Morgan didn't want to talk about it any more.

Steve got through it OK. After serving as group commander and getting his lieutenant colonelcy, he was sent home, got out of the AAF just before it became the USAF and runs a successful store in a pleasant southern town. Guppy got through it OK. His plan to drink his way out worked. He was sent home, stayed in the AAF until after the Bomb was dropped and then got out as fast as he could, shaken with fear and horror at the implications. He is now retired—a charming and urbane man who has been a leader of peace movements. He doesn't drink.

Rabbit took a GI Bill course in aeronautics and then joined the faculty of a midwestern university. He is a full professor now and takes his family on vacations with the Sierra Club.

Termite stayed in the Air Force and served in Korea, where he was shot down, escaped in a thrilling adventure, and made the cover of *Life*. He retired a few years ago and lives in Florida.

Piss-Ant fully recovered and worked out his marriage. He still sells real estate in New England.

Skunk-Ass took the GI Bill at one of the Ivy League universities, then went to Harvard Business School and made about eight million dollars in the stock market. He died in 1962 of cancer.

Jim, our first CO, stayed in the USAF and then moved onto a forty-one-foot ketch when he retired, and now lives aboard it in California. He's a total alcoholic.

Elkhart went into politics and was twice elected congressman. He lost a race for the Senate in the 1960s because his stand on Vietnam was too hawkish for a dovish constituency. He is now writing his memoirs.

Balz made it OK. He's a deacon in a Lutheran church in Tennessee.

Park made it OK. He's a journalist.

Carter shot down eight planes, knocked off six more in Korea, put in for the space program, but just missed being kept on as an astronaut because of his age. He's still with NASA, now involved with the space shuttle.

Riznik returned. After being hit that day, he bailed out and landed in swampy country with nothing around him but Japs for miles and miles. He eluded them for eight days, traveling southward by night, then was picked up by some natives. They kept him for three more days, and he realized that they were going to turn him in to the Japs for the reward. He shot four of them and escaped to a river bank, jumped in, and floated out of danger. Then he built a raft and went downstream to the coast. Here he ran into an entire Japanese regiment, swimming. He managed to keep out of sight and got through their lines that night. He traveled again by night and kept at it for five weeks. He then heard English being spoken in a clearing, peered through the brush, and found he had entered the compound of a mission station. The missionaries cared for him for two months, then contacted an American submarine, and on a dark night he was taken off by rubber dinghy. He arrived in Perth, Australia, went through rest and rehabilitation, was sent home a hero, sold war bonds, and went out with movie stars. He became a test pilot for one of the big California manufacturers, and performed beautifully until a new jet fighter blew up with him in it.

Morgan was my source for most of this. He stayed in the Air Force and retired recently, a colonel. We used to see each other when he was stationed nearby. Our wives were friends. Our kids played together.

One Armed Forces Day, we went to the Morgans for a tour of the base and a barbecue afterward. Morgan put me in the cockpit of an F-105. I found I couldn't even see ahead because the windshield was so sharp that it distorted vision.

"You use the screen," Morgan told me, leaning in. "You do everything by the screen. What you are is, you're a kind of guided missile."

I climbed out and looked at the great ugly mass of metal, designed not to fly, exactly, but to hurtle.

"Do you like it?" I asked, suddenly.

"No," he said, tersely. "The pleasure's gone out of it."

And we walked away together toward my car—a perfectly good car, but it didn't have a name.